AF690748

The Reliable Data Platform Framework

Engineering Reliable Data Pipelines and Trusted Data Products

ATTIA ELSAYED

Technics Publications
SEDONA, ARIZONA

TECHNICS PUBLICATIONS

115 Linda Vista, Sedona, AZ 86336 USA
https://www.TechnicsPub.com

Edited by Steve Hoberman
Cover design by Lorena Molinari

All rights reserved. No part of this book may be reproduced or transmitted in any form or by any means, electronic or mechanical, including photocopying, recording, or by any information storage and retrieval system, without written permission from the publisher, except for brief quotations in a review.

The authors and publisher have taken care in the preparation of this book, but make no expressed or implied warranty of any kind and assume no responsibility for errors or omissions. No liability is assumed for incidental or consequential damages in connection with or arising out of the use of the information or programs contained herein.

All trade and product names are trademarks, registered trademarks, or service marks of their respective companies and are the property of their respective holders and should be treated as such.

Without in any way limiting the author's exclusive rights under copyright, any use of this publication to "train" generative artificial intelligence (AI) technologies to generate text is expressly prohibited. The author reserves all rights to license uses of this work for generative AI training and the development of machine learning language models.

First Printing 2026

Copyright © 2026 by Attia Elsayed

ISBN, print ed. 9798898161231
ISBN, Kindle ed. 9798898161248
ISBN, PDF ed. 9798898161255

Acknowledgments

When I look back at my journey in data management, I realize this book was never just mine. It is the result of countless conversations, long nights of problem solving, moments of doubt followed by breakthroughs, and the incredible people who walked alongside me.

To the colleagues and teammates I've had the privilege of working with over the years, thank you for being my partners in discovery. Every broken job we debugged at midnight, every success we celebrated when the pipeline finally ran on schedule, every moment of frustration and relief. Those experiences became the lessons I now share in these pages. You taught me that reliability isn't just a technical standard, it's a collective responsibility.

I owe deep gratitude to my professors, leaders, and mentors who trusted me with challenges that seemed impossible at first. You pushed me to design smarter, think bigger, and never settle for "just working." Your faith in me gave me the courage to pursue excellence, even when the path wasn't clear.

To the wider data engineering community - open-source contributors, bloggers, conference speakers, and the heroes who share their wisdom freely - thank you for inspiring me daily. This book would not exist without the foundation you built.

To my family - wife, son, and daughters - thank you for your patience, love, and encouragement during this journey. Writing a book often meant stolen hours, late nights, and weekends at my desk, but you stood by me with understanding and support. Your belief in me has been the quiet force that carried me through.

I wish to express my heartfelt thanks to my father, mother, brothers, and sister for their patience, love, and encouragement throughout this journey. Your confidence in me has been the quiet, sustaining force that inspired me to keep going.

Most of all, I want to thank the next generation of data specialists. I hope that these principles help you avoid unnecessary struggles, give you confidence in your craft, and remind you that building pipelines is not just about moving data, it's about building trust.

Contents

Introduction 1

Chapter 1: Introducing the RDPF 3
The Mirage of the "Data-Driven" Enterprise 3
The Day Zero: Stepping into the Fire 5
The Fragmentation of Truth 6
The Tooling Trap 6
The Economic and Human Toll 7
The RDPF Philosophy: From Firefighter to Architect 8
Key Takeaways 9

Chapter 2: Knowing Requirements 11
The Hidden Price of Speed 11
The Strategic Compass: Why Data Needs a North Star 12
Navigating the Ecosystem: Identifying Stakeholders 13
The Discovery Workshop: Extracting the Truth 14
Defining the Finish Line: Success Metrics 16
The Requirement Contract: The Final Handshake 17
Key Takeaways 18

Chapter 3: Designing for Longevity 21
The Ghost in the Machine: The Double-Processing Disaster 21
Design as Strategy: Choosing Your Standards 23
Key Takeaways 27

Chapter 4: Choosing the Architecture 29
The Ferrari in the Driveway 29
The Right-Sizing Principle 30
Which Skeleton Fits? 31
The "Boring Technology" Rule 34
Key Takeaways 34

Chapter 5: Adopting Suitable Technology 35
The "New & Shiny" Attraction 35
The "Innovation Token" Economy 36
Build vs. Buy: The Hidden Tax 37
The Three Pillars of Technology Selection 38
Avoiding "Lock-in" without "Lock-out" 39

The "Final Handshake" with Strategy 39
Key Takeaways 40

Chapter 6: Scoping Environments 41
The "Works on My Machine" Curse 41
The Three Sites of Dev, Staging, and Prod 42
Infrastructure as Code (The Identical Twins) 43
The Data Dilemma: Realism vs. Risk 44
CI/CD: The Automated Airlock 45
Key Takeaways 46

Chapter 7: Containing Environments 47
The Mystery of the "Phantom" Failure 47
The Mirror Image: Why "Close Enough" Isn't 48
The Source of Truth: Infrastructure as Code (IaC) 49
Containerization: The Shipping Container for Code 50
Matching the Pressure: Volume and Latency Parity 50
The Immutable Infrastructure Mindset 51
Key Takeaways 52

Chapter 8: Validating Source Data 53
The Silent Killer: The Zero-Row Disaster 53
Never Trust a Stranger (Even if it's Your Own API) 54
The Quarantine Ward: Isolate, Don't Just Kill 56
Aligning the Bouncer with the Strategy 57
The Contract: Data Contracts as the Ultimate Goal 57
Key Takeaways 58

Chapter 9: Orchestrating Tasks 59
The Morning Race Condition 59
The DAG: The Law of the Land 60
The "Spiderweb" vs. The "Modular" Flow 61
Fan-In and Fan-Out: Managing the Traffic 62
The "Critical Path" and the Business Strategy 62
Retries, Timeouts, and the "Stuck" Task 63
Key Takeaways 64

Chapter 10: Ensuring Speed 65
The Query That Ate the Budget 65
The Scalability Paradox: Vertical vs. Horizontal 66
Partitioning: Finding the Needle Without the Haystack 67

The Parallelism Trap: Too Many Cooks 68
Caching: The Memory of Success 68
Performance as a Business Value 69
Key Takeaways 70

Chapter 11: Delivering on Time 71
The Midnight Ghost: A Tale of Two Time Zones 71
Event Time vs. Processing Time: The Great Illusion 72
Choosing Your Tempo: The Cost of "Real-Time" 73
The "Watermark" Strategy: Handling the Laggards 74
The SLA: A Contract with the Clock 75
Synchronization: The Silent Drifter 75
Key Takeaways 76

Chapter 12: Observing Data 77
The Dashboard of Lies 77
Monitoring vs. Observability: The "Why" Factor 78
The Three Pillars of the Unknown 79
Key Takeaways 82

Chapter 13: Detecting Errors 83
The Pager That Cried Wolf 83
The Math of Expectations: SLIs, SLOs, and SLAs 84
The Alerting Hierarchy: Triage for the Soul 85
Incident Management: The Blameless Post-mortem 86
Automated Remediation: The "Self-Healing" Alert 87
Key Takeaways 87

Chapter 14: Recovering Properly 89
The "Fat Finger" Disaster 89
Strategy 1: The Circuit Breaker (Failing Fast) 90
Strategy 2: The Automated Backfill (The Idempotency Payoff) 91
Strategy 3: Point-in-Time Recovery (PITR) 92
The "Yellow" State: Graceful Degradation 92
Key Takeaways 93

Chapter 15: Testing 95
The "Don't Touch It" Syndrome 95
The Data Testing Pyramid 96
Regression Testing: Protecting the Past 97
The CI/CD Gatekeeper (The "Airlock" Revisited) 98

Testing the "Untestable": Non-Deterministic Data 99
The Metric of Confidence: Test Coverage 99
Key Takeaways 100

Chapter 16: Building the CI/CD Pipeline 101
The Friday Afternoon Tragedy 101
CI vs. CD: The Two Halves of the Whole 102
The Anatomy of a Data Pipeline (The CI Side) 103
The Deployment Dance (The CD Side) 103
Pipeline as Code: Versioning the Process 104
Secret Management: The Invisible Shield 105
The "One-Click" Rollback 106
Key Takeaways 106

Chapter 17: Deploying 107
The "Big Bang" Bottleneck 107
Strategy 1: The "Small Batch" Philosophy 109
Strategy 2: Feature Flags (Decoupling Deployment from Release) 109
Strategy 3: The Deployment Window & The "No-Fly" Zone 110
Strategy 4: Automated Canary Testing 111
The Psychological Shift: "Boring" is Better 111
Key Takeaways 112

Chapter 18: Checking Data 113
The Double Sales Discrepancy 113
The Reconciliation Balance 114
Statistical Anomaly Detection 115
The Referential Integrity Guard 116
The "Last Mile" Circuit Breaker 116
Closing the Loop: The Data Contract Feedback 117
Key Takeaways 118

Chapter 19: Communicating with Code 119
The Legend of the "Enigma Script" 119
Readability as a Reliability Feature 120
The Linter as the Law 121
The Map of Meaning (Naming Conventions) 121
Modularization vs. The "God Script" 122
The Narrative of the Code (Commenting) 122
Key Takeaways 124

Chapter 20: Documenting 125
The "Bus Factor" Crisis 125
Documentation as Code 126
Key Takeaways 129

Chapter 21: Promoting Reliability 131
The Executive Who Wanted a "Head on a Plate" 131
The Blameless Post-Mortem 132
Key Takeaways 136

Chapter 22: Continuing Great Work 137
I. Truth Over Ease 138
II. Systems Over Heroes 138
III. Clarity Over Cleverness 138
IV. Progress Over Perfection 139
V. Empathy Over Blame 139
The End of the Journey 139

Index 141

Introduction

Every reliable data system starts with a need to solve a problem that matters, to build trust in information, and to empower people with insight.

When I first joined an organization tasked with becoming a truly data-driven company, we had a small team and massive expectations. We needed to deliver high-quality, timely data to support visualizations, reports, and machine learning across eleven markets and under tight timelines.

We couldn't afford downtime. We couldn't tolerate inconsistency. We had no room for fragile solutions.

So I set out to develop a framework that helps us consistently build reliable data pipelines: pipelines that run every day, recover from errors, validate their inputs and outputs, and scale without collapsing under the weight of success.

These principles weren't downloaded from the internet or borrowed from trendy blogs. They were extracted through real-world experience: solving late-night failures, building resilient systems, and learning the hard way what works (and what doesn't).

In this book, I've captured the principles any data engineer or team can use to build pipelines that are not just functional but also trustworthy.

You'll find a mix of practical guidance, human insight, and technical patterns. All wrapped in a style that speaks to practitioners who want to do better, not just deliver faster.

Whether you're just getting started or already managing hundreds of pipelines, I hope this book becomes your field manual: a resource you turn to when designing, debugging, or scaling your data systems.

Because in today's data-driven world, building reliable pipelines isn't optional. It's mission-critical. With the right principles, it's absolutely achievable, as experience and practice have proven.

"Reliability is the silent foundation upon which the house of Innovation is built."

Let's build with confidence.

CHAPTER 1

Introducing the RDPF

In this opening chapter, we explore the fundamental reasons why the Reliable Data Platform Framework (RDPF) is essential for modern organizations. We examine the gap between the executive vision of being "data-driven" and the operational reality of many engineering teams. We also discuss the hidden costs of unreliable systems, not just in financial terms but also in the erosion of trust and the burnout of talented engineers. Finally, we introduce the core philosophy that guides every principle in this book: reliability as a strategic necessity rather than a technical luxury.

The Mirage of the "Data-Driven" Enterprise

Every modern CEO wants their company to be data-driven. In boardrooms and investor pitches, the phrase acts as a magic spell that promises efficiency, foresight, and undisputed market dominance. The vision is always the same: a seamless flow of information where every department, from Marketing to Finance, has real-time access to a single source of truth. Decisions emerge from facts rather than gut feelings.

However, the reality is often far more chaotic. Beneath the polished executive dashboards lies an invisible refinery of tangled scripts, manual overrides, and fragile connections. When I first joined a major organization with full responsibility for Data Engineering, the gap between public ambition and internal reality felt like a canyon. The mandate from leadership was clear: rewire the company for a data-first future. But as I walked into the office, I did not see an engine of innovation. Instead, I saw a team exhausted by the weight of a system that was constantly breaking under its own success.

We often mistake having a lot of data for being data-driven.

A true data-driven culture requires more than just storage; it requires an infrastructure people trust implicitly. Without that trust, the data is just expensive noise, and the "mirage" eventually fades, leaving the business lost in the desert of misinformation.

The Day Zero: Stepping into the Fire

The first few hours at a new company usually involve HR paperwork and office tours. For the data leader, they were a step into the fire. Before even setting up the laptop, a colleague pulled into a war room. The morning's executive report showed a twenty percent drop in revenue that did not exist in reality. It was a data glitch, a silent failure in an upstream API that had gone unnoticed for forty-eight hours.

This is the Day Zero reality for many data leaders. We inherit a patchwork of infrastructure, stitched together with legacy cron jobs and scripts that just work until they do not. In this case, the team was bright and motivated but stretched thin. They spent eighty percent of their time fixing what already existed rather than building what was next. The issue was not a lack of talent; it was a lack of standards. Every team had its own way of processing data, creating a fragmented landscape where the same metric could have three different values depending on who you asked.

This audit revealed that the team lived in a permanent state of reactive firefighting. They were so busy putting out fires that they had no time to build fireproof structures. They were trapped in a cycle where every new feature added more fragility to the system.

The Fragmentation of Truth

Reliability involves more than just ensuring a job finishes. It involves ensuring that qualified data is produced and delivered correctly and on time. One of the most insidious problems I encountered was the silent failure. This is the pipeline that reports a successful status in your orchestration tool while delivering corrupted or empty tables to your users.

When truth becomes fragmented, the business loses its most valuable asset: trust. Once consumer trust is broken, it takes months of flawless performance to regain it. Fragmented truth leads to spending meetings arguing over data quality rather than discussing how to improve the business. This paralysis is the direct result of a platform that prioritizes delivery speed over content reliability.

The Tooling Trap

A common reaction to these failures is to buy more software. We tell ourselves that if we just had a better orchestrator, a faster warehouse, or a newer observability platform, the problems would vanish. But during my twenty-year career, I have seen that tools are merely force multipliers. If we use a powerful tool to automate a flawed process, we simply break things faster and on a larger scale.

The real issue is rarely a lack of tools; we often have too many. The issue is a lack of principles and standards. A reliable data platform rests on foundations such as functional isolation, idempotency, and smart recovery concepts that remain the same regardless of the specific software we use. In the early days of my transformation initiative, I realized we did not need a new tech stack. We needed a new mindset.

We needed to move away from the goal of getting it to work and toward making it bulletproof. We must treat data engineering with the same mindset that civil engineers apply to building bridges. You do not build a bridge by hoping the physics works out; you build it by calculating the load-bearing capacity and the margin for error.

The Economic and Human Toll

We often talk about data reliability in technical terms, but the human cost is what truly drives the need for this framework. Data engineering has one of the highest burnout rates in the technology sector. When pipelines are fragile, the engineers become the human glue holding them together. I have seen brilliant engineers quit because they were tired of spending their weekends debugging broken jobs that should have healed themselves. They felt like they were in a race they could never win.

Economically, the cost is even higher. Beyond the wasted salary of engineers playing firefighter, there is the cost of poor decisions. A marketing campaign based on flawed attribution data can waste millions of dollars in a single weekend. Therefore, reliability is a strategic necessity that protects both business and talent.

The RDPF Philosophy: From Firefighter to Architect

The Reliable Data Platform Framework (RDPF) was born from this chaos. It did not emerge from an ivory tower; it was forged in late-night debug sessions and high-stakes board meetings. The philosophy is simple: we assume failure is inevitable and design a system that survives it.

By following RDPF, we transition from a reactive posture to a proactive position.

We stop asking "How do I fix this?" and start asking "How do I ensure the system fixes this for me?" By the end of the transformation, we went from fighting daily fires to running over 200 pipelines worldwide that have run successfully for 1,000 days without human intervention.

This book distills those lessons into a repeatable framework. We provide a guide to building systems that never need excuses, platforms that change the way a company thinks, acts, and trusts its own information. Reliability is a culture. It lives in how we write code, how we respond to failure, and how we protect the single source of truth. We must stop reacting and start building.

Key Takeaways

- **Trust is the primary currency**: A data platform is only as valuable as the trust users place in it.
- **Avoid the tooling trap**: Principles matter more than products; automation of a bad process only creates faster failures.
- **Acknowledge the human cost**: Fragile systems lead to engineer burnout and high turnover.
- **Design for inevitable failure**: The RDPF mindset assumes the world is messy and builds self-healing systems.
- **Move beyond "just working"**: Reliability requires a shift from being a coder who solves a task to an architect who builds a resilient system.

CHAPTER 2

Knowing Requirements

Every reliable data pipeline begins not with a line of code, but with clarity. In this chapter, we explore why gathering requirements is the most critical phase of the Reliable Data Platform Framework. We move beyond simple technical specifications to understand the business intent, the origin of the data, and the cost of failure. By the end, we establish a process that ensures we build the right solution the first time, preventing the "rework cycles" that drain engineering morale.

The Hidden Price of Speed

Early in my career, a project manager approached me with what seemed like a simple request. They needed a dashboard to track daily active users across three different global regions. The deadline was tight, and the pressure was high. Driven by a desire to prove my technical speed, I skipped the deep-dive questions and started building a pipeline immediately based on assumptions.

Three weeks later, the dashboard went live. At first, there was a celebration that became a problem when the wrong numbers were revealed.

The dashboard was technically perfect,
but functionally useless.

We often mistake activity for progress. In data engineering, the "Just Build It" mentality is a recipe for technical debt. We must resist the urge to open our code editors until we can articulate the business problem as clearly as the stakeholders can. Reliability starts with a shared understanding of truth. If the foundation is based on assumptions, the entire platform will eventually lean and collapse.

The Strategic Compass: Why Data Needs a North Star

To build a truly reliable platform, we must understand the "Why" before we tackle the "How." I often see engineering teams operating in a vacuum, building over-engineered systems that serve no immediate business purpose. They build high-frequency streaming platforms when the business only needs a weekly report, or they invest millions in machine learning when the core inventory data is still fundamentally broken.

A business strategy acts as our North Star. It is the compass that dictates where we should spend engineering time. If the company's strategy for the year is "Aggressive Customer Retention," then our data activities should prioritize churn prediction, sentiment analysis, and customer support metrics. If we spend that same year optimizing the billing system for a minor efficiency gain, we have failed as we are sailing in the wrong direction.

When we align data activities with business strategy, we transform the data team from a "cost center" into a "value driver." We stop being the people who "move data from A to B" and start being the people who "enable the CEO to hit their targets." Every architectural decision we make should be a direct response to a strategic need. Without this compass, even the most reliable pipeline is just expensive plumbing.

Navigating the Ecosystem: Identifying Stakeholders

We rarely build data pipelines for our own amusement. Every byte we move serves a person or a process. To build a reliable system, we must identify two primary groups within our ecosystem: the Data Providers and the Data Consumers.

The Data Providers are the guardians of the source systems. These might be software engineers managing a production database or a marketing team handling manual file uploads. We need to understand their roadmap and consider the impacts of source action on the data pipelines to account for it.

The Data Consumers are the analysts, data scientists, and executives who rely on our output. Identifying these stakeholders early prevents requirements loss where requirements get lost in translation as they move through layers of management. We are not just moving data. We are providing a service to these individuals.

The Discovery Workshop: Extracting the Truth

Gathering requirements is an act of investigation, almost like detective work. We cannot simply wait for the ticket to arrive with a list of bullet points. We must actively seek out the truth. In my experience, the most effective way to do this is through a Discovery Workshop. This is not just another meeting on the calendar. It is a dedicated mission to align the business vision with the reality of the data.

We start by gathering the key stakeholders, whether virtually or in person, and set a clear rule: no technical debt allowed. We want to hear about business problems, not database schemas. To peel back the layers of what people *say* they want versus what they actually *need*, we use the "Five Whys" technique. If a stakeholder says, "I need a real-time table of sales," we ask why. If the answer is "to track daily performance," we ask why sub-second updates are required. Often, we find that a daily refresh is sufficient, and the "real-time" request was simply a default assumption. By digging deeper, we often save the team weeks of unnecessary, complex streaming engineering.

During these sessions, we use the "Playback Technique." After a stakeholder explains a need, we act as a mirror and repeat it back to them in our own words: *"So, if I understand correctly, you need to see the net revenue after discounts, but excluding tax, refreshed every hour so that the floor managers can adjust staffing. Is that correct?"* We wait for the nod. If they hesitate or say "well, actually," we haven't reached the truth yet. We continue this loop until the stakeholder says, *"Exactly. You've got it."*

However, workshops often reveal conflicting interests. Marketing might want a broad view of customer behavior, while Finance requires penny-perfect transaction logs. When these worlds collide, the workshop becomes a negotiation table. As data architects, we facilitate this by highlighting the trade-offs. We explain that a system designed for high-speed marketing insights might not be the same system required for financial auditing. By surfacing these conflicts early, we force the organization to make a strategic choice before we spend a single dollar on infrastructure.

We also look for the things that are so obvious to the stakeholder that they forget to mention them. For example, they might assume the data will include historical corrections for the last three years, even though the source system only keeps ninety days of logs. To catch these, we employ "Process Shadowing." We sit with the person who currently handles the data manually. We watch where they click, what Excel formulas they use, and which rows they ignore. This direct observation reveals the "mainstream knowledge" that never makes it into an official document.

Finally, we identify the "*Minimum Viable Requirement.*" We ask: "*What is the one thing this pipeline must do for you to consider this project a success?*" This helps us strip away the "nice-to-haves" and focus our engineering energy on the core value. By the end of the workshop, the fog of ambiguity should lift, replaced by a clear, documented path forward that everyone in the room has personally signed off on.

Defining the Finish Line: Success Metrics

In many organizations, "reliability" is a vague feeling.

To the RDPF, reliability must be a measurable metric. We categorize these metrics into three buckets: Availability, Accuracy, and Latency. We cannot always optimize for all three at once, so we must force our stakeholders to rank them.

I once worked with a financial firm where Accuracy was the only metric that mattered. They did not care if a report arrived three hours late, as long as every decimal point was perfect. Conversely, an ad-tech client cared only about Latency. They needed data in seconds to adjust real-time bids, even if it was only 95% complete.

When we define these success metrics at the start, we create a "definition of done." This prevents the goalposts from moving halfway through development. It also allows us to build automated checks that alert us when we fall below the agreed-upon standards. We move from guessing if a pipeline is "good" to knowing exactly how it performs against its goals.

We must act as translators. We take the high-level business logic and break it down into atomic technical steps. We use tools like flowcharts or pseudocode to convey our understanding to stakeholders.

Getting a "Yes" to that specific question saves dozens of hours of rework later. It bridges the gap between a vague KPI and a precise business requirement. When we document these definitions, we create a "Source of Truth" that prevents future arguments.

The Requirement Contract: The Final Handshake

Once we have gathered our information, we create a Requirement Contract. This is not necessarily a legal document, but a formal record of what we are building, why we are building it, and its limitations. It acts as the final handshake between the engineering team and the business.

A good contract includes the specific questions the data will answer, the agreed-upon definitions for all metrics, and the "Failure Protocol" who gets notified when things break. When a stakeholder asks for a "quick change" mid-sprint, we refer back to this contract. It protects the engineering team from scope creep and ensures the platform remains stable. A reliable platform is a predictable platform. We build with the confidence that everyone is looking at the same map.

Key Takeaways

- **Let strategy lead the way:** Use the business strategy as a compass to prioritize data projects that deliver real value.
- **Resist the urge to code immediately:** Spending time on clarity early saves weeks of rework later.
- **Master the playback:** Always repeat requirements back to stakeholders to confirm absolute alignment.
- **Shadow the user:** Watch how the business currently handles data to catch the details that documentation misses.
- **Rank your priorities:** Determine if Accuracy, Availability, or Latency is the primary driver for the project.

- **Standardize definitions:** Translate vague business terms into precise, auditable, and verifiable logic.
- **Create a contract:** Use a Requirement Contract to align expectations and protect against scope creep.

Chapter 3

Designing for Longevity

In this chapter, we move from the "What" into the "How." We explore the design principles that make a system resilient to the chaos of the real world. We discuss the holy standards of reliable design. Crucially, we examine how these technical standards must be anchored in the Business Strategy we defined in Chapter 2. By the end, you will have a set of non-negotiable standards that ensure your platform not only works but also survives reliably.

The Ghost in the Machine: The Double-Processing Disaster

There is a specific kind of cold sweat that only a data engineer knows. It usually happens around 10:00 AM on a Monday, just as the executive team is opening their weekly performance reports. I remember one such morning. Our revenue dashboard showed that we had the best sales day in the company's history, by exactly 100%.

For five minutes, the office buzzed with excitement. Had a celebrity mentioned us? Had a marketing campaign finally "gone viral"? But as I dug into the logs, the ghost revealed itself. It wasn't a sudden increase in customer numbers; it was a simple automated retry.

An upstream pipeline had timed out due to a minor network hiccup. Our orchestrator, doing exactly what it was told, triggered the job again. However, the first job hadn't actually failed; it had successfully written half its data before the connection dropped. The second job simply appended the same data again. We had "double-counted" every transaction.

Fixing it took several hours by manual deletions and a very humbling apology to the CFO. That day, I learned a painful lesson: a system that cannot handle being run twice isn't finished.

In the RDPF, we don't hope for "one-and-done" success; we design for the inevitable "try-and-try-again" reality of the cloud.

Design as Strategy: Choosing Your Standards

Before we touch a single line of code, we have to realize that every architectural choice is a business decision. If our business strategy is "Operational Excellence" (think: high-frequency trading or logistics), our design standards must prioritize latency and availability. If our strategy is "Regulatory Compliance" (think: banking or healthcare), our standards must lean heavily toward auditability and perfect accuracy.

Design standards keep the engineering team aligned with the North Star. A "Bulletproof Design" means that every pipeline follows the appropriate blueprint, ensuring that the platform's behavior is predictable for the stakeholders who rely on it. We aren't just writing code; we are building a brand of trust.

Standard #1: Idempotency (The Ultimate Safety Net)

If there is one word you should tattoo on your whiteboard, it is **Idempotency**. In plain English, an idempotent operation produces the same result no matter how many times you run it. If you run a job once, you get the result. If you run it ten times, you get the *same* result, with no duplicates and no side effects.

Think of an elevator button. If you press the button for the fifth floor once, the elevator goes to the fifth floor. If you mash the button twenty times in a fit of impatience, the elevator still just goes to the fifth floor. It doesn't go to the 100th floor or crash through the roof. That is idempotency in action.

In data engineering, we achieve this through a "Delete-then-Insert" pattern or by using "Upserts" (Update or Insert). We never just blindly append data. We design our destination tables to have unique constraints, or we check for existing data before we write. By making our pipelines idempotent, we remove the fear of the "Retry" button, knowing that the recovery is as simple as clicking "Run" again.

Standard #2: Atomicity (The "All or Nothing" Pact)

Imagine you are at an ATM. You ask for **$100**. The machine debits your bank account, but right as it's about to deliver the cash, the power goes out. If the system isn't **Atomic**, you are out $100 and have nothing to show for it.

Atomicity ensures that a transaction is a single, indivisible unit of work. Either the whole thing succeeds, or the whole thing fails. There is no middle ground. In data terms, we never want a "half-baked" table where only 50% of the rows were updated before a network glitch killed the process.

We implement atomicity using staging tables and "Atomic Swaps." We first load our data into a temporary, hidden table. We run our quality checks. Only when we are 100% sure the data is perfect do we "swap" it into the production table. This swap happens in a fraction of a second. To the end user, the data is either the old version or the new version, without the messy, half-finished process in between.

Standard #3: Functional Isolation (Stopping the House of Cards)

In a fragile architecture, everything is connected to everything else. A failure in the "Marketing" pipeline somehow causes the "Finance" dashboard to crash. This is what we call a "tightly coupled" system, and it is the enemy of reliability.

Functional Isolation is the art of building firewalls between your processes. Each pipeline should be a "black box" that handles its own logic, errors, and state. If the source API for the Weather Service goes down, it might mean our "Outdoor Sales" report is missing data, but it should never prevent the "Payroll" system from running.

We achieve this by decoupling our stages. We use a tiered structure often called a "Medallion Architecture" (Bronze, Silver, Gold), where each layer is isolated from the next. We move data into a "Landing Zone" first, then "Clean," then "Model." By isolating these functions, we ensure that a fire in one room doesn't spread to the rest of the house. It also makes debugging infinitely easier; you don't have to search the full pipeline; you just look at the failed process.

Standard #4: State Management and the "High-Water Mark"

Reliable design requires **State Management**. We use a **High-Water Mark (HWM)**. This is a simple record, usually a timestamp or an ID that tracks the last piece of data successfully processed.

When the pipeline starts, the first thing it does is ask the State Store: "*Where did I stop last time?*" If the pipeline stops at 2:00 PM and doesn't run again until 5:00 PM, it doesn't care. It starts at 2:01 PM and moves forward. This makes our systems "Time-Independent." Whether we run them every hour, every day, or once a month, they always process every single record in order. State management is the memory of your platform; without it, your pipelines have amnesia.

Standard #5: The Self-Healing Playbook

The ultimate goal of Bulletproof Design is a system that fixes itself. We move away from "Defensive Programming" (trying to prevent every error) and toward "Resilient Programming" (designing for recovery when the error inevitably occurs).

This includes:

- **Smart Retries with Exponential Backoff:** Instead of retrying every second (which can overwhelm a struggling database), we wait 5 seconds, then 30 seconds, then 5 minutes.

- **Circuit Breakers:** If a source system fails ten times in a row, the pipeline "trips the breaker" and stops, sending a high-priority alert instead of wasting resources on a dead connection.

- **Heartbeat Monitoring:** The system constantly reports "I am alive." If the heartbeat stops, the platform knows something is wrong before the data even becomes late.

When you design with these standards, the 3:00 AM pager stops being a death sentence. Most of the time, the system has already identified the failure, initiated an idempotent retry, and moved on before you've even opened your eyes.

Key Takeaways

- **Standards are the language of reliability:** Every engineer must follow the appropriate design blueprint to ensure stability across the platform.

- **Idempotency is non-negotiable:** Ensure every job can be run multiple times without side effects or duplicates.

- **Commit to Atomicity:** Use staging and swaps to ensure data delivery is an "all or nothing" pact.

- **Isolate your failures:** Decouple systems so one broken pipeline doesn't cascade through the entire platform.

- **Manage your state:** Use High-Water Marks to make your pipelines time-independent and resilient to downtime.
- **Build for recovery, not perfection:** Assume things will break and design the "Self-Healing" path directly into the code.

CHAPTER 4

Choosing the Architecture

In this chapter, we move from the abstract logic of design and into the physical structure of our platform. Architecture is the skeleton that supports your data activities. If it's too flimsy, it collapses under pressure; if it's too complex, it becomes a cage that prevents you from scaling. We will discuss the "Right-Sizing" principle, the "Boring Technology" rule, and how to navigate architectural patterns to find the one that best fits your business needs.

The Ferrari in the Driveway

A few years back, I was brought in to consult for a mid-sized retail startup. They were proud of their "bleeding-edge" stack. They had a massive Kubernetes cluster, a complex Kafka setup for real-time streaming, and a high-end graph database. It was a masterpiece of modern engineering.

They were processing about 50,000 rows of transaction data a day. To put that in perspective, you could process that entire dataset in a basic Excel spreadsheet in about four seconds. Yet, they had a team of three full-time DevOps engineers just keeping the infrastructure alive. Their pipelines crashed weekly, not because the logic was wrong, but because the architecture was so complex that no one understood how all the pieces talked to each other.

They had bought a Ferrari just to drive to the mailbox at the end of the driveway.

This is what I call Resume-Driven Development (RDD). It's the temptation to choose tools based on how cool they look on a LinkedIn profile rather than how well they solve the business problem. In the RDPF, we believe that simplicity is a reliability feature. An architecture that you can draw on a napkin and explain to a junior engineer in ten minutes will almost always outperform a "state-of-the-art" monstrosity in the long run.

The Right-Sizing Principle

Your architecture should fit your business the way a well-tailored suit fits a person. If it's too small (under-engineered), it will rip the moment you try to scale. If it's too big (over-engineered), you'll trip over the extra fabric. To "right-size" your architecture, you must look back at your Strategic Compass. Does the business actually need sub-second latency? If not, why are you building a streaming architecture that requires 24/7 monitoring? If the business only needs a daily report, a simple batch process is infinitely more reliable because it has fewer "moving parts" that can break in the middle of the night. Appropriate architecture is about Honest Engineering. It requires the courage to say, "We don't need a distributed cluster for this; a single SQL instance will handle this for the next three years." Reliability is found in the gaps between the tools. The fewer gaps you have, the less room there is for errors to hide.

Which Skeleton Fits?

Architecture isn't a one-size-fits-all uniform. To build a reliable platform, you need to select a pattern that matches your team's maturity and your data's complexity.

1. The Monolithic Pipeline (The "Quick-Start" Solution)

This is a single, unified system where ingestion, transformation, and reporting all happen in one place, either in a single database or a single giant script.

- **The Fit:** Best for **early-stage startups** or **small internal projects.** If your data volume is low and your team is just one or two people, a monolith is the most reliable choice because it has the fewest points of failure.

- **The Trap:** It doesn't scale. Eventually, one tiny bug in a marketing script brings down the entire company's reporting because everything is "tightly coupled."

2. The Medallion Architecture (The "Reliability Standard")

This pattern organizes data into layers: **Bronze (Raw)**, **Silver (Cleaned)**, and **Gold (Business-Ready)**.

- **The Fit:** Best for **mid-to-large enterprises** that need high data quality and a clear audit trail. It is the "Goldilocks" architecture. It is balanced, scalable, and resilient. It allows you to "replay" your data if something breaks, which is a cornerstone of the RDPF.

- **The Trap:** It requires more storage and more "hops" for the data. If you over-engineer the Silver layer with too many complex rules, the pipeline becomes slow and expensive.

3. The Data Mesh (The "Global Enterprise" Pattern)

Data Mesh stops treating data as a centralized lake and starts treating it as a **Product**. In this world, the team that *creates* the data (e.g., the Sales Team) is also responsible for *publishing* it in a reliable format for others.

- **The Fit:** Best for **massive, fragmented organizations** where a central team can no longer keep up with the demands of twenty different departments.

- **The Trap:** It is culturally difficult. It requires every department to have its own data engineers. Without strong central standards, a Data Mesh quickly turns into a "Data Mess."

4. The Modern Data Stack (The "Agile & SaaS" Route)

This relies on cloud-native, plug-and-play tools (like Fivetran, Snowflake, and dbt). It focuses on **ELT** (Extract, Load, and Transform) rather than the traditional ETL (Extract, Transform, and Load).

- **The Fit:** Best for **fast-growing tech companies** that need to move quickly and have the budget for SaaS tools. It's perfect for teams that want to focus on data modeling rather than managing servers.
- **The Trap:** "SaaS Sprawl." Your monthly cloud bill can explode, and you may find yourself with a "black box" where you don't actually own the underlying infrastructure.

Architecture	Complexity	Speed to Build	Cost to Scale	Best For...
Monolith	Very Low	Days	Low (initially)	Startups / Solo Projects
Medallion	High	Months	High	Enterprise Reliability
Data Mesh	Moderate	Weeks	Moderate	Global / Decentralized Teams
Modern Stack	Low	Hours	Scalable	Agile / Growth Companies

The "Boring Technology" Rule

There is a secret in high-scale engineering: the most reliable systems are built on **"boring" technology.** Boring technology is mature. It has a massive community and, most importantly, **predictable failure modes.** When a "boring" tool fails, we usually know exactly why. When a "shiny" new tool that was released recently fails, you might be the first person in the world to encounter that specific bug. In a reliable platform, we spend our "innovation tokens" wisely. If you use a brand-new database and a brand-new language, your platform becomes a lab experiment. Stick to the tried-and-true for your core infrastructure.

Key Takeaways

- **Kill the Complexity:** If a simpler tool can do the job, use it. Simplicity is the shortest path to reliability.
- **Match the Pattern to the Need:** Use the Monolith for speed, Medallion for trust, and Mesh for scale.
- **Avoid Resume-Driven Development:** Choose tools that solve problems, not ones that look good on a CV.
- **Spend Innovation Tokens Wisely:** Stick to "boring," mature technology for your core infrastructure.
- **Mind the Blast Radius:** Use bulkheads to ensure one broken part doesn't sink the ship.

CHAPTER 5

Adopting Suitable Technology

In this chapter, we move from the structural skeleton of architecture into the actual tools we use to build it. If architecture is the blueprint of a house, technology is the choice between brick, wood, or glass. We will explore why there is no such thing as a "best" tool, only the "right" tool for your specific business context. We'll dive into the Build vs. Buy debate, the true cost of "Free" open source, and how to select a stack that scales with your strategy rather than your stress levels.

The "New & Shiny" Attraction

I once worked with a team that was convinced they had found the magic tool of data processing. A new, ultra-fast distributed engine had just hit the market, claiming to be 100x faster than Spark. They spent four months migrating their entire ETL layer to this new tool. The benchmarks were, indeed, incredible. Then, the reality of production set in. Because the tool was so new, there were no connectors for their legacy databases. They had to write custom Java wrappers for everything. When a mysterious memory leak started crashing the system at 2:00 AM, there were no StackOverflow threads to help them. They were the "pioneers," which in data engineering usually means they were the ones with the guns on their heads. They chose technology based on a benchmark but forgot to check for a community.

Reliability isn't just about how fast a tool runs;
it's about how quickly you can fix it when it breaks.

We often look for a silver bullet, but end up with a lead weight. In the RDPF, we don't choose tools that look good in a keynote. We choose tools that have survived the war of production.

The "Innovation Token" Economy

Every engineering team has a limited supply of "Innovation Tokens." You only get two or three to spend on any given project. If you decide to use a brand-new, experimental database, you've spent a token. If you also use a cutting-edge, niche programming language, you've spent another. If you spend all your tokens on the infrastructure, you have none left for the actual business logic. A reliable platform is built on 80% "Boring Technology" and 20%

innovation. We use the boring stuff, such as Postgres, Python, SQL, and established Cloud providers for the heavy lifting because their failures are predictable and the community is supportive of fixing. We save our tokens for the parts of the system that provide a competitive advantage to the business. RDPF believes that technology is not a luxury; it is a tool to serve the business the best.

Build vs. Buy: The Hidden Tax

A frequent debate in technology selection is whether to build a custom solution or buy a managed service (SaaS):

- **Buying (SaaS/Managed):** You are paying for speed and reliability. You are outsourcing the "undifferentiated heavy lifting" (server patching, backup management) so your team can focus on data insights.
- **Building (Custom/Open Source):** You are choosing control and cost-efficiency. You aren't tied to a vendor's roadmap, but you now own every bug and every update.

The mistake many teams make is thinking that Open Source is "free." Open source is only free if your engineers 'time has no value. If you spend $50,000 a year on a managed ingestion tool, it might feel expensive until you realize it would cost $200,000 in engineering salaries to build and maintain a custom version that is only half as reliable. In the RDPF, we prioritize **Time to Value.** If buying a tool gets the data into the hands of decision makers six months faster, the tool has already paid for itself.

The Three Pillars of Technology Selection

When evaluating a new piece of technology, we run it through the "RDPF Filter." If it doesn't pass all three pillars, it doesn't enter our stack.

1. Interoperability (Does it play well with others?)

Data engineering is a team sport. Your transformation tool needs to talk to your orchestrator, which needs to talk to your monitoring suite. If a tool requires you to build "custom bridges" for every connection, it is a liability. We favor tools with open APIs, standard SQL interfaces, and native connectors for the major cloud ecosystems.

2. The Talent Market (Can I hire for this?)

This is the most "human" part of the technology selection process. You can build the most elegant system in the world using an obscure functional programming language, but if you can't find engineers to maintain it, the system will eventually die. A reliable platform is one that can be handed off. If the primary architect leaves, the platform shouldn't collapse. We choose technologies that have a healthy, growing pool of talent.

3. Operational Observability (Does it talk to me?)

A suitable technology must have "first-class" logging and metrics. If a tool hides its inner workings in a "black box," it is a threat to your reliability. We look for tools that export logs to standard formats (like JSON) and integrate with modern observability platforms (like CloudWatch).

Avoiding "Lock-in" without "Lock-out"

There is a fear in our industry of "Vendor Lock-in," which means that if you use too many features from a specific vendor, you can never leave. While this is a valid concern, many teams over-correct by building "Vendor Agnostic" layers that are so complex they become a "Lock-out." They spend so much time trying to make their code work on every cloud provider that they never actually make it work well on any of them.

In the RDPF, we accept a degree of strategic lock-in in exchange for reliability. If technology provides a feature that prevents data loss, we use it. We document the lock-in and ensure that our Business Strategy justifies the trade-off.

The "Final Handshake" with Strategy

Finally, your technology must match the "speed of the business."

- If you are a **High-Growth Startup**, you need "Low-Code/No-Code" tools that allow you to pivot in days.
- If you are a **Fortune 500 Bank**, you need "High-Control" tools with rigorous security and auditing capabilities.

Using a "Startup Stack" in a bank will get you fired for security breaches. Using a "Bank Stack" in a startup will kill the company because you'll move too slowly. The technology is only "suitable" if it empowers the strategy we defined in Chapter 2.

Key Takeaways

- **Beware the Silver Bullet**: No tool solves every problem. Focus on community and support over benchmarks.
- **Spend Innovation Tokens Wisely**: Use boring technology for 80% of your stack to ensure predictability.
- **Account for the "Engineer Tax"**: Open source isn't free; factor in the cost of maintenance and mental overhead.
- **Prioritize the Talent Pool**: Only choose tools you can actually hire people to run.
- **Demand Observability**: If a tool doesn't export clear logs and metrics, it doesn't belong in a reliable platform.
- **Accept Strategic Lock-in**: Don't let the fear of vendors prevent you from using features that actually improve reliability and the business.

CHAPTER 6

Scoping Environments

In this chapter, we move from the "what" of technology into the "where." Even the most perfectly written code is a liability if it's running in the wrong place. We explore the necessity of isolated environments (Dev, Staging, and Production), and why "testing in prod" is the fastest way to burn out your team and lose your stakeholders' trust. By the end, you'll learn how to build a series of airlocks that ensure your experiments stay in the lab and only "proven truth" reaches the business.

The "Works on My Machine" Curse

Early in my career, I spent three days perfecting a complex transformation script. On my local machine, using a small sample of data, it was a work of art. It was fast, the logic was sound, and the output was beautiful. With a triumphant click, I pushed the code directly to the production server. Ten minutes later, the entire platform ground to a halt.

My local machine had 16GB of RAM and was processing a few thousand rows. The production server was trying to move ten billion rows through a network bottleneck I hadn't accounted for. Worse yet, the production data contained "Null" values in a field my local sample promised would always be populated. My "artistic" script crashed, leaving the company's main sales table in a corrupted, half-finished state.

I had committed the fatal mistake of data engineering: I treated "Production" like a playground. I learned that day that reliability isn't just about the code you write; it's about the **environment** that code lives in.

If you don't have a place to fail safely,
you will eventually fail publicly.

The Three Sites of Dev, Staging, and Prod

On a reliable platform, we treat our environments like high-security biohazard labs. You don't test a new vaccine by injecting it into the general population; you start in a laboratory, move to a controlled trial, and only then release it to the world.

- **Development (The Sandbox):** This is your laboratory. It's where you are free to break things, experiment with new libraries, and write messy code. Here, you use "mock" data or a tiny, anonymized sample of real data. The goal here is **iteration speed**. If the server smokes, no one dies, and no dashboards turn red.

- **Staging (The Rehearsal):** This is the most underrated environment. Staging must mirror Production. It should have the same hardware, the same security permissions, and a full (or near-full) volume of data. If your code survives Staging, you have a 90% chance it will survive the real world. This is where you catch the "OOM" (Out of Memory) errors, semantic exceptions, and the weird data edge cases.

- **Production (The Holy Site):** This is where the business lives. No human should ever manually run code here. No one should "quick-fix" a table in the middle of the night via a terminal. Changes only arrive here through an automated, tested deployment pipeline.

By isolating these "failure domains," we ensure that our mistakes have a "blast radius" of zero.

Infrastructure as Code (The Identical Twins)

The biggest threat to isolated environments is "Environment Drift." This is when someone manually tweaks a setting in Production but forgets to do it in Staging. Suddenly, your "mirror" is distorted. You test in Staging and it passes, but it fails in

Production because a single configuration flag is different. To solve this, we use Infrastructure as Code (IaC).

Instead of clicking buttons in a cloud console to create a database, we write a script using tools like Terraform that describes exactly what the environment should look like. We use the *same script* to build Dev, Staging, and Prod. This ensures that our environments are identical twins. If a piece of code works in the "Twin A" (Staging), we have mathematical certainty that it will work in "Twin B" (Production).

The Data Dilemma: Realism vs. Risk

The hardest part of isolation in data engineering is the data itself. To have a reliable Staging environment, you need "real" data to test against. But using real production data in a lower environment is a massive security risk. If a developer accidentally leaks the Staging database, they've leaked the company's secrets.

We handle this through **Data Masking and Anonymization**. We build a "bridge" that pulls data from Production into Staging, but as it crosses the bridge, we scrub it. Names become "User A," "User B." Credit card numbers become a string of "X's." Salaries are shifted by random percentages.

This gives us the **volume** and **variety** of production data (to test performance and edge cases) without the **liability** of production data. Reliability means protecting the customer's privacy as fiercely as we protect the pipeline's uptime.

CI/CD: The Automated Airlock

In the RDPF, we don't move code between environments by hand. We use **Continuous Integration and Continuous Deployment (CI/CD)**. Think of this as an automated airlock to control the flow of code from Dev to Staging, then to production.

When a developer finishes their work in Dev, they "submit" it to the airlock. The CI system immediately runs a battery of automated tests. If a single test fails, the airlock door to Staging stays locked. If it passes, the code is automatically deployed to Staging. Once it passes the "Rehearsal" in Staging, a senior engineer (or a final automated check) clicks a button to move it into Production.

This removes human error from the equation. We don't have to remember which file to copy or which password to use. The process is **predictable, repeatable**, and **boring.** And in data engineering, "boring" is the highest compliment you can pay a system.

Key Takeaways

- **Production is Holy:** Never, ever work directly in Production. If you don't have a Staging environment, you are testing in Prod by default.
- **Mirror the Reality:** Your Staging environment must be as close to Production as possible—hardware, volume, and permissions.
- **Automate the Build:** Use Infrastructure as Code to ensure your environments don't "drift" apart over time.
- **Mask the Secrets:** Use anonymized data in lower environments to balance testing realism with security.
- **The Airlock Principle:** Use CI/CD to move code between environments. If it isn't automated, it isn't reliable.

CHAPTER 7

Containing Environments

In the previous chapter, we built the barriers that separate our playground from our holy site. But a barrier is useless if the specifications inside it are fundamentally different from those in the playground. In this chapter, we explore the art of ensuring that your Dev, Staging, and Production environments are not just isolated, but identical. We will discuss the "Shadow Bug," the power of Infrastructure as Code (IaC), and why "similar" is the most dangerous word in a data engineer's vocabulary.

The Mystery of the "Phantom" Failure

I once worked on a high-stakes migration for a global logistics firm. We had spent days testing our new data warehouse in the Staging environment. We ran millions of records through it, stress-tested the API calls, and even simulated a partial network outage. In Staging, the system was perfect. It was fast, reliable, and passed every validation gate.

Confident, we flipped the switch to Production. Within twenty minutes, the system started throwing "Connection Reset" errors. But it wasn't happening to every record, only about 5% of them.

We spent forty-eight hours in a "War Room," hunting for a bug that didn't seem to exist. The code was identical. The data was identical. The database version was identical. Finally, we found the culprit: a tiny, hidden configuration setting on the Production load balancer that timed out connections 10 seconds faster than the one in Staging. That 10-second difference was the "Shadow Bug." It only appeared under the specific network conditions of the Production environment. We had built a "similar" production environment, but we hadn't built an **identical** one. In the RDPF, "similar" is a trap.

If your environments aren't identical twins, your testing is just a sophisticated form of guessing.

The Mirror Image: Why "Close Enough" Isn't

In data engineering, we often settle for "close enough." We use a smaller database instance in Staging to save money, or we use a slightly older version of a library because "it's basically the same."

This is a recipe for disaster. Data platforms are sensitive to their surroundings. A slight difference in a Python version can change how a timestamp is parsed. A difference in available RAM can change how a Spark job shuffles data. A different cloud region can introduce latent network "jitters" that cause an API ingestion script to crash.

To build a reliable platform, you must enforce **Environmental Parity**. This means that from the OS kernel up to the application code, everything should be a mirror image. If Production has 64GB of RAM and uses Python 3.11.4, Staging must have 64GB of RAM and use Python 3.11.4. Reliability is the daughter of consistency.

The Source of Truth: Infrastructure as Code (IaC)

How do you ensure two complex cloud environments stay identical? You don't do it by hand. Human beings are terrible at repetitive consistency; we get bored, skip steps, and make typos. We solve this using **Infrastructure as Code (IaC)**. We treat our servers, databases, and networks like software. Instead of clicking buttons in a web console, we write scripts using tools like Terraform that define the "State" of our world. When we need to update a database setting, we change the code in our IaC repository. We then "apply" that code to Dev, then Staging, and finally Production. The code becomes the **Single Source of Truth** for the environment. If it's written in the script, it exists in the world. This eliminates "Configuration Drift" and any slow, silent misalignment that happens when people make "quick tweaks" to one environment but forget the others.

Containerization: The Shipping Container for Code

Before the 1950s, loading a ship was a nightmare. Sacks of grain were piled next to barrels of oil. Every ship was packed differently, and things broke constantly. Then came the **Shipping Container,** which became a standard box that fits on every ship, every truck, and every crane in the world. In our world, **Docker** is that shipping container.

By "containerizing" our data pipelines, we package the code, the libraries, the configuration, and the operating system into a single, immutable box. We run that exact same box in Dev, Staging, and Production. This solves the "Works on My Machine" problem forever. The code doesn't care if it's running on a developer's laptop or a massive Kubernetes cluster in the cloud; the environment inside the container is always the same.

Matching the Pressure: Volume and Latency Parity

The most common place where "Similar" environments fail is in **Scale**. A pipeline that works perfectly with 1,000 rows might behave completely differently with 1,000,000,000 rows. In Staging, your joins might take seconds; in Production, they might cause the database to run out of temporary disk space and crash.

To be truly reliable, you must perform **Volume Testing** in Staging. You don't necessarily need to keep 100TB of data in Staging 24/7 (that's expensive), but you should have the ability to "spin up" a full-scale dataset for a performance test before a major release.

You also need **Network Parity**. If your Production environment is behind a strict corporate firewall or uses a specific VPN, your Staging environment must live behind that same firewall. You want to find the network bottlenecks during your "rehearsal" in Staging, not during the "opening night" in Production.

The Immutable Infrastructure Mindset

In the cloud days, we don't "fix" a server that is misbehaving; we terminate it and spin up a new one from our IaC script. This is called **Immutable Infrastructure**.

If an environment feels "weird" or "glitchy," we don't spend hours debugging the configuration. We wipe it clean and redeploy the entire stack from our code. This ensures that we are always running on a "Known Good State." It removes the "ghosts" that accumulate in long-running systems, ensuring that our environments remain mirrors of our intent.

Key Takeaways

- **"Similar" is a Danger Sign:** Aim for absolute parity. Small configuration differences cause the most expensive failures.
- **Codify Your World:** Use Infrastructure as Code (IaC) to ensure your environments are predictable and repeatable.
- **Containerize Everything:** Use Docker to ensure the code's immediate surroundings never change, regardless of where it's running.
- **Test the Scale:** Ensure your Staging environment can handle the volume and network constraints of Production.
- **Embrace Immutability:** Don't patch environments; redeploy them. This keeps the "Mirror of Truth" clear and free of configuration drift.
- **Automate the Mirror:** Use your CI/CD pipeline to push infrastructure changes through the environments just like you push code.

CHAPTER 8

Validating Source Data

In this chapter, we transition from the "where" of our infrastructure to the "who" of our data. If your platform is a high-end banking system, your source data is the crowd trying to get in. Some are VIPs, but many are troublemakers looking to start a fire. We explore the **Bouncer Pattern**, the "Trust but Verify" mindset, and the specific gates every piece of data must pass before it's allowed to touch your clean, reliable tables.

The Silent Killer: The Zero-Row Disaster

I'll never forget the "Black Friday" of 2019. We were expecting record-breaking data volumes. The engineering team was on high alert, staring at CPU monitors and memory graphs. Everything looked green. The pipelines were running too fast. By noon, the

Marketing Director stormed into our room. "Why does the dashboard say we've made $0 today?"

We checked the logs. The pipeline had been "successfully" completed in record time. Why? Because the source API had changed its authentication protocol that morning without telling us. Instead of an error, it simply returned an empty list: []. Our pipeline, being a "good soldier," processed that empty list, wiped the "Current Sales" table to prepare for the new data, and committed the change. We hadn't "failed." We had "succeeded" in deleting our company's most important real-time data.

That was my introduction to the **Silent Killer**. A system that only monitors for "crashes" is blind to the most dangerous type of failure: **bad data in a good pipeline.** In the RDPF, we don't assume the source is telling the truth. We treat every incoming file like a suspicious package.

Never Trust a Stranger (Even if it's Your Own API)

The most common mistake in data engineering is the "Assumption of Sanity."

We assume the upstream software team won't rename a column. We assume the third-party API won't suddenly start sending temperatures in Fahrenheit instead of Celsius.

A reliable platform is built on **Defensive Ingestion.** We implement three distinct "Gated Checks" at the very edge of our platform, empowered by the airlock between the messy outside world and our clean internal architecture.

Gate 1: The Passport Check (Schema Validation)

Before we even look at the data values, we look at the structure. Does the file have the 12 columns we expected? Is "User_ID" still an Integer, or did it suddenly become a String containing "Unknown"?

We use **Schema Enforcement** at the point of entry. If the "Passport" doesn't match our records, the bouncer denies entry immediately. We don't try to "cast" the data or "fix" it on the fly. We stop the process and alert the source owner. This prevents "Schema Drift" from poisoning your downstream models.

Gate 2: The Expiry Date (Freshness & Latency)

Data has a shelf life. If you are a logistics company, data that is three hours old might be useless. If you are a financial firm, data that is three minutes old might be dangerous. Every ingestion must include a **Freshness Check.** We look at the maximum timestamp in the incoming batch. If the "current" data is actually from yesterday, the bouncer flags it. This prevents the old data from being reprocessed as new, resulting in confusing business logic.

Gate 3: The Weight Check (Volume & Statistical Profiling)

This is where we catch the "Zero-Row Disaster." We compare the incoming batch to historical norms.

- "We usually get 10,000 rows on a Tuesday. Today we got 50."
- "The average 'Transaction_Amount' is usually $45. Today it's $4,500."

If the data is outside of these **Standard Deviations**, it's held for review. We don't necessarily kill the pipeline, but we flag it as "Suspicious." This is the difference between a reactive team (finding out from the CEO) and a proactive team (finding out from the bouncer).

The Quarantine Ward: Isolate, Don't Just Kill

When the bouncer finds a troublemaker, they don't just shut down the entire system. They pull that person aside so the work can continue. In a fragile system, a data quality error can kill the entire pipeline. In an RDPF system, we use the **Quarantine Pattern.**

We split the stream. The "Good" records continue to the Silver layer. The "Bad" records (those that failed validation) are redirected to a **Quarantine Table.** This allows the business to see

95% of the data immediately while the engineering team investigates the 5% that failed. This maintains **Availability** without sacrificing **Accuracy.**

Aligning the Bouncer with the Strategy

How strict should your bouncer be? This goes back to Chapter 2.

- **The "Strict" Bouncer (High-Accuracy Strategy):** In a banking system, a single bad record kills the batch. Accuracy is the North Star.
- **The "Friendly" Bouncer (High Availability Strategy):** In a social media sentiment tracker, we can lose 1% of the data as long as the dashboard keeps moving.

Your source checks must be configurable. We don't hard-code "Strictness" into the pipelines; we define it in our **Metadata Store.** This allows the business to tune the "Quality Gates" as the strategy evolves.

The Contract: Data Contracts as the Ultimate Goal

The ultimate evolution of source checks is the **Data Contract.** This is a formal agreement between the "Producer" (the team creating the data) and the "Consumer" (you).

It's no longer just a technical check; it's a professional practice. The Producer promises to provide data in a specific format, and you promise to process it. If they break the contract, *their* system should fail before the data even reaches you. While source checks protect you from the symptoms, Data Contracts are the cure for the disease.

Key Takeaways

- **Trust Nothing:** Assume all source data is "guilty" until proven "innocent" by your validation gates.
- **Monitor the Vitals:** Check for Schema, Freshness, and Volume in every single batch.
- **Silence is Deadly:** A pipeline that finishes successfully with zero rows is a failure in disguise.
- **Use the Quarantine Ward:** Isolate bad data so the rest of the business can keep moving.
- **Align with the Strategy:** Your validation "strictness" should reflect the business's tolerance for risk.
- **Work Toward Contracts:** Turn technical checks into organizational agreements to stop errors at the source.

CHAPTER 9

Orchestrating Tasks

In this chapter, we move from the individual "building blocks" of data to the **orchestration** required to make them dance. A data platform isn't a single event. It is a complex series of interconnected events. If your design is sheet music, Task Dependency is the conductor, ensuring the violins don't start before the cellos. We will explore the "Spiderweb" effect, the power of the **Directed Acyclic Graph (DAG)**, and how to manage the critical path. Hence, your platform stays reliable even when the "orchestra" is thousands of tasks deep.

The Morning Race Condition

I once worked on a reporting suite for a digital marketing agency. Every day at 9:00 AM, performance managers review the insights from marketing campaign performance to improve. One day, the report showed a 0% conversion rate for generated leads into appointments. At first glance, they thought the data pipeline had crashed and that the report was outdated. The reality was much more mundane: a **Race Condition**.

The "Report Generator" task had started exactly at 5:45 AM, as scheduled. However, the "Data Ingestion" task in the CRM system, which usually took 10 minutes, had encountered a minor delay and was still running. The report didn't fail, but it simply processed an empty table. We had built a **Schedule**, not a **Pipeline**.

A schedule says, "Do this at 5:00 PM." A pipeline says, "Do this only *after* the previous task has successfully finished." In the RDPF, we never rely on clocks. We rely on **dependencies**.

If you don't respect the order of operations, you aren't building a platform; you're playing a high-stakes game of "Musical Chairs" where the losers are your stakeholders.

The DAG: The Law of the Land

To manage dependencies, we use the **Directed Acyclic Graph (DAG)**. It sounds like a mouthful, but the concept is the foundation of modern data orchestration.

- **Directed:** The data flows in one direction (A leads to B).

- **Acyclic:** There are no loops. (Task A cannot depend on Task B if Task B also depends on Task A).
- **Graph:** A map of relationships.

The DAG is your platform's "Order of Operations." It ensures that your **Silver** layer isn't processed until the **Bronze** layer is validated, and your **Gold** layer doesn't update until the Silver layer is pristine. By explicitly defining these relationships, we remove the "guessing game" from the platform. If the first domino doesn't fall, the rest of the line stays standing.

The "Spiderweb" vs. The "Modular" Flow

As a platform grows, dependencies tend to turn into a "Spiderweb" where everything is connected to everything else. In a spiderweb, a failure in the "Marketing" task can unexpectedly halt the "Financial" report due to a hidden, undocumented dependency.

To maintain reliability, we practice **Dependency Decoupling**. Instead of one giant DAG that manages every task in the company, we build **Modular DAGs**. We use **Sensors** or **Events** to signal between them.

- **The Ingestion DAG** finishes and "emits" a signal.
- **The Transformation DAG** "listens" for that signal.

This creates a "Bulkhead" (as we discussed in Chapter 4). If the Ingestion DAG fails, the Transformation DAG simply waits. It doesn't crash; it doesn't process bad data; it just stays in a holding pattern until the signal is clear.

Fan-In and Fan-Out: Managing the Traffic

In a reliable platform, you will often encounter two patterns:

- **Fan-Out:** A single ingestion task finishes, and ten different transformation tasks start simultaneously to process that data for different departments.
- **Fan-In:** Multiple source systems (Sales, Web Traffic, Weather) must all finish before a "Master Business Report" can be generated.

Managing these requires **Atomic Orchestration**. If you have a "Fan-In" where three sources are required, but only two show up, a reliable platform must know how to wait. We use "Wait-for-All" logic to ensure we never provide a partial picture of the truth. Reliability is found in the **patience** of your orchestration.

The "Critical Path" and the Business Strategy

Not all dependencies are created equal. This is where we return to the **Business Strategy** from Chapter 2.

If your strategy is "Financial Compliance," the tasks leading to the end-of-month balance are on the **Critical Path**. These tasks should have the highest priority in your orchestrator. If the system is under heavy load, the orchestrator should "starve" non-essential tasks (such as "Internal Blog Analytics") to ensure the Critical Path has the resources it needs to finish on time.

Dependency management is the technical means by which we enforce business priorities. By tagging our tasks with **Priority Weights**, we ensure that the most important data is always the first to arrive at the finish line.

Retries, Timeouts, and the "Stuck" Task

What happens when a dependency is never met? A source system goes offline, and your pipeline is left waiting forever. This is where **Timeouts** and **Dead-Letter Alerts** come in.

A reliable task dependency doesn't just wait; it has a **boundary**. If a dependency isn't met within a specific window (e.g., 2 hours), the orchestrator "trips the circuit breaker." It stops waiting, alerts the engineering team, and potentially triggers a "Fallback" task, perhaps using yesterday's data to provide a "placeholder" report so the business isn't left completely in the dark.

Key Takeaways

- **Clocks are Liars:** Never use time-based schedules for dependent tasks. Use explicit links.
- **Respect the DAG:** Ensure your data flow is a one-way street with no circular loops.
- **Decouple with Signals:** Use sensors and event-based triggers to keep your DAGs modular and maintainable.
- **Identify the Critical Path:** Prioritize tasks that support the primary business strategy.
- **Design the "Wait" Logic:** Use timeouts and fallback patterns so a single missing dependency doesn't freeze the entire platform.
- **Fan-In with Care:** Ensure "Master" reports wait for *all* sources to be validated before running.

CHAPTER 10

Ensuring Speed

In this chapter, we move from the foundational "safety" of our platform into its "speed." Many engineers make the mistake of chasing performance too early, building a race car before they've even learned how to steer. In the RDPF, we believe that **Performance is a sub-function of Reliability.** A pipeline that processes a billion rows in ten seconds is useless if five of those rows are wrong. But once the trust is built, speed becomes our greatest asset. We will explore the mechanics of horizontal scaling, the art of partitioning, and why "efficiency" is often the difference between a profitable platform and a bankrupt one.

The Query That Ate the Budget

I once witnessed a "performance disaster" that had nothing to do with a crash and everything to do with efficiency. We had a junior analyst who wrote a SQL query to join two massive tables, "Users" and "Events." On his local machine, it worked in three seconds.

He pushed it to production. Because he hadn't used an indexed Join Key and hadn't filtered by date, the database attempted a "Cross Join." For three hours, the cloud warehouse churned through trillions of permutations and used a significant amount of compute credits.

The query was "reliable" in the sense that it would have eventually finished and given the correct answer. But it wasn't **Performant**. It was an unguided missile. This is why high performance isn't just a "nice to have." It is a financial and operational guardrail. In the RDPF, we don't just ask, "Can it run?" We ask, "Can it run without burning the house down?"

The Scalability Paradox: Vertical vs. Horizontal

When a system slows down, the instinctive reaction is to "throw more hardware at it." This is known as **Vertical Scaling** (or "scaling up"). You buy a bigger server with more RAM and CPU.

Vertical scaling is easy, but it has a "ceiling." Eventually, you reach the biggest machine money can buy, and you still have more data to process. Reliability at scale requires **Horizontal Scaling** ("scaling out"). Instead of one giant horse pulling a heavy wagon, you use a team of twenty smaller horses.

In data engineering, this means using distributed systems like Spark, Snowflake, or BigQuery. These systems break a single massive task into a thousand tiny "sub-tasks" and process them in parallel. If one "horse" in the team trips, the others keep pulling. This is the heart of high-performance reliability: **Redundancy through Distribution.**

Partitioning: Finding the Needle Without the Haystack

The secret to high performance isn't processing data faster; it's **processing less data.** Imagine a library with ten million books. If you want to find a book about "Beekeeping," you don't start at the first shelf and read every spine. You go to the "Science" section, then the "Biology" aisle, then the "Insects" shelf. This is **Partitioning**. In a high-performance platform, we partition our data by common access patterns such as date, region, or department. When a query asks for "Sales in New York for yesterday," the system uses **Partition Pruning**. It ignores 99.9% of the data and only "scans" the tiny slice that matters.

The formula for performance efficiency can be thought of as:

$$E = D_{total} / D_{scanned}$$

The higher the ratio of total data to scanned data, the more performant (and cheaper) your platform becomes.

The Parallelism Trap: Too Many Cooks

If one chef can bake a cake in an hour, can sixty chefs bake a cake in one minute? Of course not. In fact, sixty chefs in one kitchen would likely result in a cake made of salt and a trip to the emergency room.

In data pipelines, **Parallelism** is a double-edged sword. If you split a task into too many pieces, the "overhead" of managing those pieces, talking across the network, and shuffling data between nodes, takes longer than the actual processing. This is called **Resource Contention**.

A high-performance RDPF platform uses **Adaptive Concurrency**. We don't just set "Parallelism = 100" and hope for the best. We monitor the "Shuffle Write" and "Network Wait" metrics. If the system is spending more time "talking" than "doing," we scale back. True performance is about finding the **Sweet Spot** where work is distributed but communication is minimal.

Caching: The Memory of Success

In many companies, the same "Executive Dashboard" is refreshed a hundred times a day. If your platform recalculates the "Total Revenue" from scratch every time someone hits "Refresh," you are wasting millions of cycles.

We use **caching** to store the results of expensive computations.

- **At the Database Layer:** We use materialized views.
- **At the Application Layer:** We use tools like Redis.
- **At the BI Layer:** We use "extracts" rather than live queries.

By "remembering" the answer to a question, we provide sub-second latency to the user while keeping our heavy-duty compute engines idle. This is the **Strategy of Least Effort**, and it is the hallmark of a mature, high-performance architecture.

Performance as a Business Value

Finally, we must align our speed with our **Business Strategy**.

- **Low Latency Strategy:** If you are building a fraud detection system, performance is measured in **milliseconds**. You will spend more money on "Hot Storage" and "In-Memory" processing because the cost of being slow is higher than the cost of the hardware.
- **High Throughput Strategy:** If you are building an end-of-year audit report, performance is measured in **terabytes per hour**. You don't care if the first row takes ten minutes to arrive, as long as all ten billion rows arrive by morning.

We don't build "fast" systems; we build **"Appropriately Fast"** systems. We use our performance metrics to ensure we are meeting the Service Level Agreements (SLAs) we promised the business in Chapter 2.

Key Takeaways

- **Reliability First, Speed Second:** Never optimize a broken process. Fix the logic, then make it fast.
- **Scale Out, Not Up:** Use distributed architectures to avoid the "vertical ceiling" and increase redundancy.
- **The Best Data is No Data:** Use partitioning and pruning to minimize the amount of data your engines have to touch.
- **Beware the Overhead:** Don't over-parallelize. Manage the "communication cost" between your nodes.
- **Cache the Truth:** Use materialized results to save money and provide "instant" answers to repetitive questions.
- **Measure the "Right" Speed:** Align your performance tuning with the specific latency requirements of your business strategy.

CHAPTER 11

Delivering on Time

In this chapter, we move from the "how fast" of performance into the "when" of delivery. Timing in a data platform is like the heartbeat of a marathon runner: it must be steady, predictable, and perfectly synchronized with the body's needs. We will explore the differences between Event Time and Processing Time, the high-stakes trade-offs between Real-time and **Batch**, and why a clock that is off by just one second can cost a business millions. By the end, you'll learn that in the world of reliability, "on time" is the only time that matters.

The Midnight Ghost: A Tale of Two Time Zones

Early in my career, I managed global sales reporting for a massive e-commerce brand. Every morning at 8:00 AM GMT, the executive team would look at the "Previous Day's Total Revenue."

For months, the system was flawless. Then, we expanded into the US market. Suddenly, the Tuesday morning report showed 50% decrease in sales KPI. The managing director was on the phone, raised the flag, and asked for an explanation. Every pipeline had finished successfully. The data was there. The transformations were correct. So, where was the money?

The culprit was a **Temporal Mismatch**. The London servers were running on UTC, the New York sales were recorded in EST, and our daily "snapshot" was triggered at midnight UTC. Because we hadn't accounted for the 5-hour lag, the "Tuesday" report was cutting off the most profitable hours of the New York Monday evening. The money wasn't gone; it was just "trapped" in the wrong day.

This is the **Midnight Ghost**. It's the error that only appears when the sun goes down in one place and rises in another. I learned that day that Time is not a universal constant in data engineering; it is a variable that must be managed precisely.

Event Time vs. Processing Time: The Great Illusion

The most dangerous trap in timing is confusing **when something happened** with **when you found out about it**.

- **Event Time:** The moment the customer actually clicks "Buy" on their phone in a subway in Tokyo.

- **Processing Time:** The moment that data finally reaches your cloud warehouse after sitting in a queue for three hours.

If you build your reports based on **Processing Time**, your data is a fiction. If your ingestion pipeline goes down for four hours and then recovers, all those Tokyo sales will appear to have happened simultaneously when the system came back online. Your "hourly sales" graph will show a flat line followed by a massive, fake spike.

Reliability requires **Event-Time Processing**. We must design our systems to "wait" for late-arriving data and place it in the correct historical bucket. This is harder to build, but it's the only way to ensure the platform tells the truth.

Choosing Your Tempo: The Cost of "Real-Time"

Every business leader *says* they want real-time data. It sounds exciting. It sounds modern. But in the RDPF, we ask: *"Does the business actually make decisions in real-time?"*

There are three primary "tempos" for data delivery, and each has a different reliability profile:

- **Batch (The Daily Pulse):** Data moves once a day or once an hour. It is the most reliable because you have the "whole picture" before you start. It's cheap, predictable, and easy to fix if it breaks.

- **Micro-Batch (The Heartbeat):** Data moves every 1–15 minutes. This is the "Goldilocks" zone for most businesses. It feels fast enough for operational monitoring but still allows for the "Atomic Swaps" we discussed in Chapter 3.

- **Streaming (The Constant Flow):** Data moves in milliseconds. This is the "Formula 1" of data engineering. It is incredibly complex and brittle. A single network jitter can cause "out-of-order" events that ruin your aggregations.

If your strategy is "Operational Awareness," you might need Streaming. But if your strategy is "Quarterly Financial Reporting," Streaming is a massive, unnecessary risk. **The most reliable timing is the slowest one the business can tolerate.**

The "Watermark" Strategy: Handling the Laggards

In a distributed world, data is rarely punctual. A mobile app might lose connection in a tunnel and upload its data three hours late. How does your pipeline know when it's "safe" to close the books for an hour and send the report?

We use **Watermarks**. A Watermark is a moving threshold that says, *"I will wait for data up to 10 minutes late. Anything older than that will be processed in a 'Late Arrivals' bucket."* Watermarking is the "patience" of your platform. It prevents the system from rushing to a conclusion with incomplete data. Without a watermark strategy, your reports will constantly "flicker," showing one number at 9:00 AM and a different number at 10:00 AM for the same time period. Flicker kills trust and watermarks build it.

The SLA: A Contract with the Clock

Timing is the only part of a data platform that is explicitly "Contractual." In Chapter 2, we defined our **Service Level Agreements (SLAs)**. An SLA isn't just a goal; it's a promise.

If your SLA says "Data will be fresh within 15 minutes," and your pipeline takes 14 minutes to run, you are living on the edge of disaster. A reliable platform maintains a **"Timing Buffer."** If the business needs data in 15 minutes, we design the system to deliver it in 5. This 10-minute buffer is our "safety margin" for when a server reboots or a source API slows down.

Synchronization: The Silent Drifter

Finally, we must address **Clock Drift**. In a cloud environment, thousands of different servers are all keeping their own time. If Server A thinks it's 12:00:01 and Server B thinks it's 11:59:59, your "Atomic Swaps" can fail, or your dependencies can trigger in the wrong order.

We ensure reliability by using **Network Time Protocol (NTP)** to sync all servers to a single atomic clock and, more importantly, by using **Centralized Orchestration**. We never let an individual server decide when to start a job based on its internal clock. We let the Orchestrator (the Conductor we met in Chapter 9) send the "Start" signal based on a single, unified truth.

Key Takeaways

- **Time Zones are Not Optional:** Always store and process data in UTC, and only convert to local time at the very last step of visualization.
- **Event Time is Truth:** Always anchor your logic to when the event happened, not when the data arrived.
- **Don't Over-Stream:** Choose the slowest tempo that satisfies the business strategy to minimize complexity and cost.
- **Respect the Laggards:** Use Watermarks to handle late-arriving data without "flickering" your reports.
- **Build a Timing Buffer:** Your pipeline execution time should be significantly shorter than your business SLA.
- **Centralize the Clock:** Never trust individual server clocks; rely on a central orchestrator to maintain the rhythm.

CHAPTER 12

Observing Data

In this chapter, we reach the critical stage of our journey: **Visibility**. If your platform is a high-speed train, observability is the cockpit, the sensors on the tracks, and the communication line to the station. We explore why "Green Dashboards" can often be the biggest liars, the difference between monitoring and observability, and how to build a system that tells you *why* it's broken before you even have to ask.

The Dashboard of Lies

A few years ago, I walked into a "War Room" where a major financial service was dealing with a massive data discrepancy. The CTO pointed at a screen filled with glowing green lights. "Every monitor we have says the system is 100% healthy," he said, his voice trembling with frustration. "But our quarterly revenue report is missing $10 million. If the system is healthy, where is the money?"

The problem wasn't that they weren't watching their system; it was that they were watching the **wrong things**. They had plenty of **Monitoring** and knew the CPUs weren't melting and the databases were "up." But they had zero **Observability**. They couldn't see *inside* the data pipelines to understand the state of the data as it transformed.

It turned out that a silent logic error in a "Tax Calculation" script was rounding numbers down to the nearest dollar rather than the nearest cent. Over millions of transactions, that tiny "cent-bleed" became a $10 million hole. The system was "up," but the data was dying. In the RDPF, we don't just care if the engine is running; we care if the pipeline is actually delivering the data to the right destination.

Monitoring vs. Observability: The "Why" Factor

People often use these terms interchangeably, but they are fundamentally different:

- **Monitoring:** Tells you *that* something is wrong. ("The pipeline failed.")
- **Observability:** Tells you *why* it is wrong. ("The pipeline failed because the 'Tax_Rate' column received a Null

value from the Singapore API, which caused the division function to crash.")

Monitoring is reactive; it's a red light on the dashboard. Observability is proactive; it's the flight data recorder that allows you to reconstruct the entire journey.

To build a reliable platform,
you need to move beyond "uptime" and into "insight."

The Three Pillars of the Unknown

To achieve true observability, your platform must emit three types of signals:

- **Metrics (The Vitals):** These are the numbers. CPU usage, row counts per hour, and latency. Metrics are great for spotting trends and triggering alerts.
- **Logs (The Diary):** These are the stories. "User A started job," "Connection timed out," "Retrying in 5 seconds." Logs give you the context behind the metrics.
- **Traces (The Map):** In a modular architecture, a single piece of data might travel through five different services. A "Trace" follows that data from start to finish, showing you exactly where the delay or the error occurred.

The Five Pillars of Data Observability

While software engineering focuses on the "Three Pillars" above, data engineering requires a specific set of lenses to look at the **data itself**. We call these the "Five Pillars of Data Observability":

Pillar	Question It Answers	Example Failure
Freshness	Is the data up to date?	The daily sales report hasn't been updated in 36 hours.
Volume	Did we get the expected amount?	We usually get 1M rows; today, we got 100.
Distribution	Does the data look "normal"?	90% of our customers are suddenly listed as "Age: 0."
Schema	Did the structure change?	A "Phone_Number" column was renamed to "Contact_Info."
Lineage	Where did this come from?	"Who calculated this 'Profit' column and what was the formula?"

Without these five pillars, you are flying blind. You might have the fastest, most "performant" system in the world, but if you aren't observing the data's health, you are just delivering useless data at the speed of light.

Alerting with Empathy: Avoiding "Alert Fatigue"

The greatest enemy of a reliable platform is the "Boy Who Cried Wolf." I have seen teams that receive 500 automated Slack alerts a day. Do you know what they do with those alerts? They ignore them.

Alert Fatigue is a reliability killer. If your observability framework screams about every tiny hiccup, your team will eventually miss the grand failure because it was buried under a pile of "Low Disk Space" warnings.

In the RDPF, we use **Actionable Alerting**:

- **Critical Alerts:** Go to a pager. These are "Service is Down" or "Data is Corrupted" events that require immediate human intervention.
- **Warnings:** Go to a Slack channel. These are "Performance is dipping" or "Small volume dip" events that should be checked during business hours.
- **Informational:** Stay in the logs. These are "Job finished successfully" or "Auto-retry succeeded" events that we only look at when debugging.

Lineage: The Map of Accountability

The most advanced piece of the observability puzzle is **Lineage**. This is a visual map that shows the life of a data point from the moment it was born in a source database to the moment it appears on the dashboard.

When a stakeholder says, "This number looks wrong," lineage allows you to work backward. You can show them exactly which table provided the data, which ingestion script moved it, and which source API provided the original value. Lineage doesn't just fix bugs; it **builds trust**. It proves to the business that you have full control over the "Mirror of Truth."

Key Takeaways

- **Monitoring is not enough:** You need to know *why* things are happening, not just *that* they are happening.
- **Watch the Data, Not Just the Servers:** Implement the Five Pillars (Freshness, Volume, Distribution, Schema, Lineage).
- **Emit Clear Signals:** Ensure every task in your DAG (Chapter 9) produces logs and metrics.
- **Kill the Noise:** Audit your alerts regularly. If an alert doesn't require a specific action, it shouldn't be an alert.
- **Use Lineage for Trust:** Being able to "prove" where a number came from is the ultimate reliability feature.
- **Stay Proactive:** Use observability to find the "cent-bleeds" before they become "$10 million holes."

CHAPTER 13

Detecting Errors

In this chapter, we move from the "seeing" to the "acting." We explore the psychology of the "On-Call" engineer, the mathematical precision of **SLIs** and **SLOs**, and how to design an alerting system that people actually respect rather than resent. We will discuss the "Signal-to-Noise" ratio and the art of the **Blameless Post-mortem**. By the end, you'll learn that the goal of alerting isn't just to find errors. It's to reduce the "Mean Time to Recovery" (MTTR) while keeping your team's sanity intact.

The Pager That Cried Wolf

I oncc joined a team where the primary "Alerting Strategy" was a shared Slack channel called #data-emergency. This channel received over 1,200 notifications a day. Most were things like *"Job 'X' retrying for the 1st time"* or *"Latency slightly above 95th percentile."* Do you know what the engineers did? They muted the channel.

One Tuesday, the main production database ran out of storage and stopped accepting new data. The alert fired, buried deep between two notifications about a minor API lag. No one saw it for six hours. By the time they did, the company had lost a significant number of transactions.

The team hadn't failed because they lacked alerts. They failed because they had **too many**. In the RDPF, an alert that doesn't require immediate action is **noise**.

Noise is the primary enemy of reliability because it masks the red flags.

The Math of Expectations: SLIs, SLOs, and SLAs

To alert effectively, you must first define what "Good" looks like. We use three levels of measurement to turn business strategy into technical triggers:

- **Service Level Indicator (SLI):** The specific metric you are measuring (e.g., "The percentage of successful pipeline runs").
- **Service Level Objective (SLO):** The target value for that metric (e.g., "99.5% of pipeline runs must succeed").

Service Level Agreement (SLA): The business contract. If the SLO is missed, what is the consequence? (e.g., "We refund the client 10% of their fee.")

The Alerting Hierarchy: Triage for the Soul

A reliable data platform categorizes its "cries for help" into three distinct buckets. If you treat every paper cut like a heart attack, your team will burn out in months.

Level	Channel	Definition	Action Required
P0: Critical	Pager/Phone	The "Golden Signals" are failing. Data is being lost or is massively corrupted.	Immediate intervention (24/7).
P1: Warning	Dedicated Slack	SLO is at risk. Performance is degrading, but data is still flowing.	Investigation within business hours.
P2: Info	Logs/Dashboard	Scheduled jobs finished, minor retries occurred.	No immediate action; used for weekly audits.

Every alert that reaches a human must pass the **"So What?" Test.** If an engineer looks at an alert and says, "Okay, so what?," the alert is poorly designed. A reliable alert must contain three things:

- **The What:** What exactly is broken? (e.g., "The Revenue Ingestion Pipeline has stalled").
- **The Impact:** Who is affected? (e.g., "The Finance Dashboard is showing four-hour-old data").
- **The Playbook:** How do I fix it? (A link to a specific document detailing the steps to restart the service or clear the cache).

If you don't provide a **Playbook Link** in the alert, you are forcing a sleep-deprived engineer to solve a puzzle at 3:00 AM. That is not a strategy for reliability. It's a recipe for human error.

Incident Management: The Blameless Post-mortem

When a major alert fires and an incident occurs, the work isn't done when the "Green Light" returns. In the RDPF, every P0 incident must end with a **Blameless Post-mortem**.

The goal is not to find out *who* broke the system. The goal is to determine why the system broke.

- *"Why did our Staging environment (Chapter 6) not catch this?"*
- *"Why did our Data Quality Gate (Chapter 8) let this through?"*
- *"How can we automate the fix so this alert never has to fire again?"*

Reliability is a **learning loop**. You use your alerts to find the holes in your armor, and then you patch them.

Automated Remediation: The "Self-Healing" Alert

The ultimate goal of Chapter 13 is to put the bouncer (from Chapter 8) to work. If an alert fires because a service is "Stuck," why wait for a human to log in and restart it?

We implement **Automated Remediation**.

- **Alert:** "Memory usage on Node A is 95%."
- **Action:** The system automatically spins up Node B and drains the traffic from Node A.
- **Notification:** "I was feeling sick, so I replaced myself. Check the logs when you have a chance."

This is the peak of the RDPF. We don't just alert on problems. We build systems that can perform "First Aid" on themselves while we sleep.

Key Takeaways

- **Noise is a Threat:** If an alert doesn't require a specific, immediate action, it should not be a P0 alert.

- **Respect the Error Budget:** Tie your alerting logic to your SLOs. Save the "Fire Alarms" for when the house is actually on fire.
- **Provide the Playbook:** Never send an alert without a link to the instructions on how to fix it.
- **Be Blameless:** Focus on system failures, not human mistakes, during post-mortems.
- **MTTR is the North Star:** Your alerting framework exists to reduce the time to return to "Green."
- **Automate the "Easy" Fixes:** Use your alerts to trigger self-healing scripts whenever possible.

CHAPTER 14

Recovering Properly

In this chapter, we reach the final stage of technical maturity in the RDPF. We've built the eyes to see (Observability) and the nerves to feel (Alerting). Now we build the **willpower** to recover. Smart Recovery isn't just about fixing a bug. It's about the system's ability to restore itself to a known "Good State" with minimal human intervention and zero data loss using the art of the **Automated Backfill.**

The "Fat Finger" Disaster

I once watched a senior engineer try to "manually" recover a corrupted table during a high-pressure outage. He was tired, his hands were shaking slightly, and he was typing SQL commands directly into a production terminal. He meant to run a SQL statement without an appropriate WHERE clause.

In one keystroke, he didn't just delete the "bad" data; he deleted the entire history of the company's sales. The "recovery" had become a second, much larger disaster. This is why, in a reliable platform, **manual recovery is a last resort.** If you haven't scripted your recovery, you haven't finished building the feature. Smart Recovery means moving the "human" out of the danger zone and letting the code handle the cleanup.

In the RDPF, we follow different strategies to facilitate data-smart recovery. We don't just use backups. We use **Active-Active** replication.

Strategy 1: The Circuit Breaker (Failing Fast)

Borrowed from the world of electrical engineering and microservices, a **Circuit Breaker** prevents a small failure from cascading into a total system meltdown.

Imagine your pipeline is pulling data from a third-party API that is currently struggling. If your pipeline keeps hammering that API with retries, the API might block your IP address, or your pipeline might stay "stuck" for hours, hogging resources.

A Smart Recovery system "trips" the breaker. It says: *"The API has failed 5 times in a row. I am going to stop trying for 30 minutes."* During that time, the platform enters a **Degraded State**. It might show "Yesterday's Data" on the dashboard with a "Maintenance" flag. This is "Smart" because it conserves your resources and protects the upstream system while the environment heals.

Strategy 2: The Automated Backfill (The Idempotency Payoff)

This is where Chapters 3 and 6 (Idempotency) finally pay their dividends. In a fragile system, if you miss three days of data, you have to manually calculate which files are missing and write a custom "one-time" script to load them.

In a Smart Recovery system, you use **State-Based Backfilling.** The system looks at the "Target" table and the "Source" folder, identifies the gap, and automatically triggers the pipeline for the missing dates.

- **Step 1:** Detect the "Data Hole."
- **Step 2:** Clear the "half-baked" data using the Delete-then-Insert pattern.
- **Step 3:** Re-run the standard pipeline logic.

Because the pipeline is **Idempotent**, the system doesn't care if it's running for "Today" or "Last Tuesday." The logic is the same, and the result is guaranteed to be consistent.

Strategy 3: Point-in-Time Recovery (PITR)

Sometimes the data isn't missing; it's just **wrong**. Maybe a bad transformation logic was deployed, corrupting the last 24 hours of data.

Smart Recovery utilizes **Point-in-Time Recovery**. If you are using modern cloud warehouses (like Snowflake, BigQuery, or Databricks), you have "Time Travel." You can query the table exactly as it existed at 2026-03-08 10:00:00. Recovery becomes a simple "Clone" command:

CREATE TABLE sales_restored CLONE sales AT (TIMESTAMP => '2026-03-08 10:00:00')

This is the ultimate safety net. It allows you to "Undo" a human error or a logic bug in seconds rather than hours.

The "Yellow" State: Graceful Degradation

The most "reliable" platforms intend to spend time 95% "Green," 4% **"Yellow,"** and 1% "Red."

- **Green:** All data is fresh and accurate.
- **Yellow:** The main pipeline is delayed, but the "Fallback" pipeline is providing estimated data.
- **Red:** The system is completely offline.

Smart Recovery aims to stay in the "Green" and shorten "Yellow" and "Red" time as long as possible. If your main source fails, do you have a secondary source? If your high-performance cluster is down, can you run a "light" version of the report on a smaller database? This is **Graceful Degradation**, and it proves that you value the user's experience over technical perfection.

Key Takeaways

- **Script the Cure:** If a recovery step is manual, it is a liability. Automate your "Fix-it" scripts.
- **Trip the Breaker:** Don't let a failing dependency sink your entire platform.
- **Leverage Time Travel:** Use Point-in-Time recovery features to "Undo" logic errors instantly.
- **Embrace the "Yellow":** Design for partial success. It is better to give the business a "Good Guess" than a "Blank Screen."
- **The Idempotency:** Use your idempotent design to make backfilling automatic.

CHAPTER 15

Testing

In this chapter, we move from the "Reactive" measures of alerting and recovery into the "Proactive" shield of **Automated Testing**. If the previous chapters taught us how to survive a crash, this chapter teaches us how to prevent the collision in the first place. We will explore the **Testing Pyramid**, the difference between **Code Tests** and **Data Tests**, and why Test-Driven Development (TDD) is the only way to scale a platform without scaling your anxiety.

The "Don't Touch It" Syndrome

I once consulted for a global bank that had a "Risk Calculation" script that was over 10,000 lines of SQL. It was written in 2012 by an engineer who had long since left the company. No one on the current team understood how it worked, but everyone knew it was the most important script in the building. Whenever a stakeholder asked for a small change, the lead engineer would go into panic mode. "We can't touch that," he would whisper. "If we change one line, the whole thing might collapse, and we won't know it's broken until the regulators call us three months from now."

This is **The "Don't Touch It" Syndrome**. It is the ultimate sign of a fragile platform. When you are afraid to improve your code, your platform is effectively dead; it's just waiting for the environment to change enough to kill it. **Automated Testing is the cure for this fear.** It turns "I hope this works" into "I know this works."

The Data Testing Pyramid

In traditional software, we have a "Testing Pyramid." In the RDPF, we adapt this to include the unique challenges of data.

1. Unit Tests (Testing the Logic)

These are the smallest, fastest tests. They test a single function in isolation using "Mock Data."

- **Example:** If I pass a price of $100 and a tax rate of 10% into my calculate_total function, does it return exactly $110?
- **The Goal:** To ensure the **Math** is right before it ever sees a real database.

2. Integration Tests (Testing the Handshake)

These tests ensure that the different parts of your platform are talking to each other correctly.

- **Example:** Can my ingestion script successfully write a file to the S3 bucket? Does the transformation script have the permissions to read from the "Bronze" table?
- **The Goal:** Ensure the **Plumbing** is leakproof.

3. Data Quality (DQ) Tests (Testing the Reality)

Unique to data engineering, these tests check the *output* of the code against business rules.

- **Example:** "The 'Percentage_Score' column must never contain a value greater than 100." or "The 'Email' column must follow a valid email regex."
- **The Goal:** To ensure the **Truth** is maintained even when the logic is "technically" successful.

Regression Testing: Protecting the Past

The most common way a platform breaks is when a new feature accidentally destroys an old one. This is why we use **Regression Testing**.

Every time you find a bug and fix it, you must write a test to ensure that specific bug **never comes back.** Over time, you build a "Wall of Protection" around your platform. A year from now, a new junior engineer might try to change a logic that seems "inefficient," and your regression test will immediately fire an alert: *"Stop! This logic exists because of a weird edge case in the 2024 Tax Law. Do not change it."* Testing isn't just for the present; it's a way of **communicating with your future self.**

The CI/CD Gatekeeper (The "Airlock" Revisited)

In Chapter 6, we talked about the "Airlock" of isolated environments. Automated Testing is the **security guard** inside that airlock. When you "Push" a code change, the CI (Continuous Integration) server should automatically:

- Spin up a temporary, clean environment.
- Run every single Unit and Integration test.
- Run a "Sample" pipeline on a small dataset.
- Only if **100% of tests pass**, allow the code to move to Staging.

By automating this, you remove the "Human Factor." You no longer have to "remember" to run the tests. The system refuses to function without them. This is the **Discipline of Automation.**

Testing the "Untestable": Non-Deterministic Data

A common excuse for not testing data platforms is: *"The data is always changing; I can't write a test for something I can't predict."* This is a misunderstanding of what a test is. You don't test for "The Answer"; you test for the **"Boundaries of Sanity."**

- You can't predict exactly how much revenue you'll make tomorrow, but you can test that it isn't a **negative number**.
- You can't predict exactly how many users will sign up, but you can test that the signup_date is **not in the future**.

We use tools like dbt-tests to define these "Sanity Boundaries." If the data crosses the line, the test fails, and the pipeline trips the Circuit Breaker (Chapter 14).

The Metric of Confidence: Test Coverage

How much testing is enough? We measure this through **Test Coverage**. While 100% coverage is often an unrealistic "vanity metric," you should aim for **100% Critical Coverage**.

Component	Criticality	Target Coverage
Financial Calculations	Vital	100 %
PII/Security Logic	Vital	100 %
Marketing Attribution	High	80 %
Internal Lab Projects	Low	20 %

By focusing your testing efforts on the "Strategic Compass" (Chapter 2), you ensure that the most important parts of your platform are the most protected.

Key Takeaways

- **Kill the Fear:** Automated testing gives you the "Permission to Change." Without it, your platform will eventually become a legacy anchor.
- **Build the Pyramid:** Use Unit tests for logic, Integration tests for connections, and DQ tests for business truth.
- **Tests are Documentation:** A well-written test tells the next engineer exactly what the code is *supposed* to do.
- **Automate the Guard:** Never deploy code manually. Let the CI/CD pipeline be the final judge of quality.
- **Test the Boundaries:** You don't need to predict the data to test its "Sanity."
- **Focus on the Vital:** 100% coverage is a myth; 100% **Critical** coverage is a requirement.

CHAPTER 16

Building the CI/CD Pipeline

In this chapter, we take everything we've built: the code, the tests, the environments, and the recovery logic. All of these components are placed onto the **Conveyor Belt of Automation**. We move from the "Craftsman" phase of data engineering into the "Industrial" phase. We will explore the mechanics of **Continuous Integration (CI)** and **Continuous Deployment (CD)**, the "Airlock" revisited, and how to perform seamless rollouts that make "Downtime" a relic of the past.

The Friday Afternoon Tragedy

We've all been there. It's 4:30 PM on a Friday. A stakeholder needs a "tiny" fix in a transformation script. You make the change locally, it looks good, and you manually upload the file to the production server. You close your laptop and head home. By 6:00

PM, the production database had crashed because that "tiny" fix contained a typo in a configuration path that exists only in the production environment.

In a fragile system, **human intervention is the single greatest risk.** Every time a human touches a production environment, there is a non-zero chance of catastrophe. In the RDPF, the CI/CD pipeline is our way to prevent a catastrophe. It ensures that the path from a developer's brain to the production server is filtered through a series of cold, impartial, and perfectly consistent machines.

CI vs. CD: The Two Halves of the Whole

While often grouped together, CI and CD serve two distinct roles in the reliability lifecycle:

- **Continuous Integration (CI):** Focuses on the **Developer**. It's the process of automatically merging code into a shared repository, running the **Auto-Tests** from Chapter 15, and building the "Artifact" (the Docker container or the Zip file).

- **Continuous Deployment (CD):** Focuses on the **Environment**. It's the process of taking that tested artifact and automatically moving it through Dev, Staging, and Production.

The Anatomy of a Data Pipeline (The CI Side)

A reliable CI process acts as a **Quality Filter**. When a developer submits a "Pull Request," the CI pipeline should trigger a sequence that looks like this:

- **Linting:** The system checks for "clean code." Are there trailing spaces? Are variables named according to our standards? It sounds petty, but clean code is easier to debug during a 2:00 AM incident.
- **Unit & Integration Tests:** As discussed in Chapter 15, the CI server runs every test. If a single test fails, the pipeline halts. No exceptions.
- **The Build:** The system compiles the code and packages it. In modern data stacks, this usually means building a **Docker Image**. This image is the "Immutable Box" we discussed in Chapter 7.
- **Static Analysis:** The system scans for security vulnerabilities. Is there a hard-coded password in the script? Is a library out of date?

By the time the code reaches a human for "Review," it has already been vetted by a machine that never gets tired and never misses a typo.

The Deployment Dance (The CD Side)

Once the code is integrated and tested, the CD side of the pipeline takes over. In a reliable platform, we don't just "overwrite" the old version with the new one. We use sophisticated deployment strategies to minimize risk.

1. Blue-Green Deployment

You run two identical production environments: "Blue" (the current version) and "Green" (the new version). You deploy the new code to Green, run a few "Smoke Tests" to ensure it's healthy, and then simply flip a "switch" (usually a Load Balancer or a DNS record) to point all traffic to Green. If something goes wrong, you flip the switch back to Blue instantly.

2. Canary Deployment

Named after the "Canary in the Coal Mine," this strategy involves rolling out the change to a tiny subset of your data or users first (e.g., 5%). You monitor the **Observability Framework** (Chapter 12) for errors. If the "Canary" stays healthy for an hour, you roll it out to the rest of the platform.

Pipeline as Code: Versioning the Process

A common mistake is building your CI/CD pipeline by clicking buttons in a web interface (like Jenkins or GitHub Actions). This creates "Hidden Magic," as nobody knows exactly how the deployment works because it's buried in a UI that isn't accessible to everyone.

In the RDPF, we use **Pipeline as Code**. Your deployment logic lives in a text file (like pipeline.yaml) right next to your data scripts. This means:

- **The pipeline is versioned:** If someone breaks the deployment process, you can "Roll Back" the pipeline itself.
- **The pipeline is transparent:** Any engineer can read the file and understand exactly what tests are being run and where the data is being moved.

Secret Management: The Invisible Shield

A pipeline needs passwords to talk to your databases and APIs. One of the most common causes of a data breach is an engineer accidentally committing a "Secret" (an API key or password) to the code repository.

A reliable CI/CD pipeline uses **Secret Injection**. The code contains a "placeholder" (e.g., ${DB_PASSWORD}), and the CI/CD system injects the actual password from a secure "Vault" (like AWS Secrets Manager) at the very last second. This ensures that no human nor log file ever sees the raw credentials.

The "One-Click" Rollback

The true test of a CI/CD pipeline isn't how it deploys; it's how it **undeploys**. In a reliable platform, "Rolling Back" to the previous version should be as easy (and fast) as deploying the new one. Because we use **Immutable Artifacts** (containers) and **Infrastructure as Code**, a rollback is simply telling the system: *"Stop running Version 2.0 and start running Version 1.9 again."* This should take seconds, not hours, to restore data pipeline reliability.

Key Takeaways

- **Eliminate Manual Steps:** If you have to type a command to deploy, you have a point of failure.
- **CI is for Quality, CD is for Safety:** Use CI to filter out bugs and CD to manage environment transitions.
- **Automate the "Mirror":** Use Blue-Green or Canary deployments to ensure failures have a small blast radius.
- **Codify the Process:** Store your pipeline logic in your repository to version and audit it.
- **Protect the Secrets:** Never put passwords in your code; let the pipeline "inject" them from a secure vault.
- **The Rollback is the Priority:** Design your pipeline so that "Going Back" is the easiest thing you can do.

CHAPTER 17

Deploying

In this chapter, we move from the "how" of automation to the "when" of strategy. Automation (Chapter 16) is the engine, but deployment timing is the steering wheel. Shipping code too slowly leads to "Release Bloat" and stagnation. Shipping too quickly without a rhythmic pulse leads to chaos and "Change Fatigue." We will explore the DORA metrics for data, the power of feature flags, and why the most reliable teams are those that turn deployment into a non-event through consistent, timely cadences.

The "Big Bang" Bottleneck

Let's assume there is a retail giant that follows a "Monthly Release" cycle. They only deployed once every 30 days, regardless of whether it was a critical security patch or a minor color change on a dashboard. All changes had to wait for the "Monthly Train."

By the time the release window opened, the "Train" had 400 different code changes from 50 different engineers. The deployment took 12 hours. Because so much was changing at once, something *always* broke, and with 400 changes, finding the culprit was like looking for a needle in a haystack made of needles.

The fear of breaking the system led them to deploy less frequently, which made each deployment larger and more likely to break. It was a death spiral of reliability. In the RDPF, we break this cycle by recognizing that safety lies **in frequency, not in hesitation.**

To measure if our deployment is "Timely," we use the four DORA (DevOps Research and Assessment) metrics, adapted for the data world:

1. **Deployment Frequency (DF):** How often do we ship code to production? (Target: Daily or multiple times a week).

2. **Lead Time for Changes (LT):** How long does it take from "Code Finished" to "Data Flowing in Prod"?

3. **Change Failure Rate (CFR):** What percentage of deployments result in an incident?

4. **Mean Time to Recovery (MTTR):** When a deployment fails, how fast can we get back to "Green"?

The relationship between deployment frequency and platform stability is a direct relationship. High frequency leads to higher stability because if a "tiny" change breaks the system, the fix is obvious and immediate.

Several strategies can be used to achieve timely deployment without disrupting data platform stability. These strategies are explained in the following sections.

Strategy 1: The "Small Batch" Philosophy

Timely deployment requires an obsessive focus on small, atomic changes. Instead of building a "Whole New Warehouse" and shipping it in six months, we ship the "Customer Table" this week, the "Orders Table" next week, and the "Revenue Logic" the week after.

This reduces the **Cognitive Load** on the team. When you deploy a small change, you can hold the entire logic in your head. If the monitoring turns red, you know exactly which three lines of code caused the issue. Timeliness is not about rushing; it's about reducing the weight of the cargo so the ship can move faster.

Strategy 2: Feature Flags (Decoupling Deployment from Release)

This is the "Secret Weapon" of modern reliability. A **Feature Flag** is a simple conditional switch in your code that lets you deploy code to production while keeping it "Off" for users.

By using feature flags, you can ship code on a Tuesday morning (when the whole team is awake and caffeinated) but not "Turn it On" until Friday afternoon. This allows you to test the code in the production environment with real data volumes without affecting the final dashboards. You have "Deployed" the code, but you haven't "Released" the feature yet.

Strategy 3: The Deployment Window & The "No-Fly" Zone

While we want to deploy frequently, we must respect the **Context of the Business**. Deploying a major change to the sales pipeline at 4:55 PM on the last day of the fiscal quarter is not "Agile."

A reliable platform defines **Deployment Windows**:

- **Green Zones:** High-coverage hours when the full engineering team is available to respond to incidents.
- **No-Fly Zones:** Critical business periods (e.g., Black Friday, Board Meetings, End-of-Month, Before Weekends, and Public holidays) where only emergency "Hotfixes" are allowed.

Timely deployment means being fast enough to serve the business but disciplined enough to stay out of the business's way during high-stakes moments.

Strategy 4: Automated Canary Testing

As we touched on in Chapter 16, a timely deployment is one that "proves itself." In a **Canary Release**, the CI/CD pipeline automatically deploys the new code to a "Shadow" table. The system then compares the "New Result" to the "Old Result."

If the variance is less than 1%, the deployment automatically continues to the rest of the platform. This is **Automated Validation**. It removes the "Wait for Human Review" bottleneck, allowing the platform to maintain a high cadence without sacrificing the "Bouncer" (Chapter 8) at the gate.

The Psychological Shift: "Boring" is Better

The ultimate goal of timely deployment is to make the process **Boring**. If your team feels a spike of adrenaline or anxiety every time they hit "Deploy," your process is not yet reliable.

When you deploy small changes every day, the "Risk per Deployment" drops so low that it becomes routine, like checking email. This cultural shift is the "Final Boss" of the RDPF. Reliability is not a state of perfection. It is a state of **predictability**.

Key Takeaways

- **Frequency is a Safety Feature:** Smaller, more frequent deployments reduce the "Blast Radius" of errors.
- **Adopt DORA:** Measure your success by how fast you can move from "Idea" to "Production Data."
- **Flag Everything:** Use feature flags to separate the *technical* act of deploying from the *business* act of releasing.
- **Respect the Business Cycle:** Establish "No-Fly Zones" for critical periods to avoid unforced errors.
- **Automate the Comparison:** Use "Canary" logic to let the data prove the code is safe.
- **Aim for Boredom:** If deployment is a high-drama event, your batch sizes are too big.

CHAPTER 18

Checking Data

In the earlier chapters, we built bouncers at the source and airlocks in the pipeline. But there is one final, critical frontier: the **Destination**. This is the data that the CEO, the algorithms, and the customers actually see. Even if your source was clean and your code was perfect, things can go wrong during the final "placing" of the data. We will explore **Reconciliation**, **Anomaly Detection at Rest**, and the **"Last Mile" Circuit Breaker**.

The Double Sales Discrepancy

I once witnessed a total platform meltdown that had nothing to do with a crash. The ingestion was green. The transformations were green. But when the Finance team looked at the "Final Monthly Revenue" table, it showed double sales. The code hadn't failed. It had performed a "Cross Join" that accidentally doubled the worth of transactions.

The pipeline did exactly what it was told, but the **Destination** was a lie. This is why we need Destination Data Checks. If Source Checks are the bouncer at the door, Destination Checks are the food safety inspector who checks the meal right before it leaves the kitchen. If the plate isn't perfect, it doesn't matter how clean the ingredients were.

The Reconciliation Balance

The most fundamental check at the destination is the **Balance Sheet**. In accounting, every debit must have a credit. In data engineering, every row in must have a corresponding result out.

We use a simple **Reconciliation Formula** to ensure no data was "lost in translation":

$$R_{count} = I_{rows} - (Q_{rows} + D_{rows})$$

Where:

- R_{count} is the final record count at the destination.
- I_{rows} is the initial input count.
- Q_{rows} are the rows intentionally quarantined (Chapter 8).

- D_{rows} are the rows intentionally dropped (e.g., filtered duplicates).

If the math doesn't balance, the Destination Check fails. This prevents "Silent Data Loss" from reaching your stakeholders.

Statistical Anomaly Detection

Sometimes the row counts match, but the **values** are insane. This is where we move from "counting" to "profiling." A reliable destination check looks at the **distribution** of the data.

- **The "Zero-Value" Check:** Did the "Average Order Value" suddenly drop from $50 to $0.05?
- **The "Null-Spike" Check:** Did a column that is usually 99% populated suddenly become 40% Null?
- **The "Volume-Shift" Check:** Did we unexpectedly process 5x as much data as on any other Tuesday in history?

We treat these as "Suspicious" flags. A Destination Check shouldn't just look for "Broken" data; it should look for "Weird" data.

The Referential Integrity Guard

In modern distributed databases, we often lose the "Hard Constraints" (Foreign Keys) that protected us in the old days of SQL. It is very easy to end up with "Orphaned Records" such as sales that belong to a non-existent store, or clicks that belong to a deleted user.

A Destination Check runs a **Referential Audit**:

1. Scan the final "Gold" tables.
2. Check for any ID that doesn't exist in its respective "Dimension" table.
3. If orphans are found, the check flags the data as **"Integrity Compromised."**

Check Type	What it Protects	Level of Alert
Row Count	Completeness	P0 (Critical)
Mean/Max/Min	Accuracy	P1 (Warning)
Null Percentage	Validity	P1 (Warning)
Referential Match	Consistency	P0 (Critical)

The "Last Mile" Circuit Breaker

This is the ultimate expression of the RDPF. We don't just "check" the data and send an email; we **block the view**.

If a Destination Check fails, the system triggers a **Visualization Circuit Breaker**.

- Instead of showing a wrong number on the CEO's dashboard, the dashboard displays a "Data Under Maintenance" banner.
- The API stops serving the "Current" table and falls back to the "Last Known Good" snapshot.

It is always better to provide no data than to provide wrong data. Providing wrong data leads to bad business decisions but providing no data leads to an engineering ticket. One costs millions; the other costs a few hours of work.

Closing the Loop: The Data Contract Feedback

Destination checks shouldn't just be the end of the line; they should be the beginning of the next cycle. When a Destination Check fails, the "Metadata" about that failure is fed back into the **Observability Framework** (Chapter 12).

This allows us to ask: *"If the destination is wrong, but the source was 'clean,' which transformation logic in Chapter 10 needs to be adjusted?"* This turns your destination into a **Quality Feedback Loop** that constantly hardens the entire platform.

Key Takeaways

- **Check the Pipeline:** Perfect code can still produce wrong results due to data context.
- **Balance the Books:** Use the Reconciliation Formula to ensure zero silent data loss.
- **Watch for "Weird":** Use statistical profiling to catch anomalies that pass schema checks but fail the "Sanity Test."
- **Audit Your Links:** Regularly check for orphaned records to maintain referential integrity.
- **Break the View:** If the data is wrong, hide it. Never let a stakeholder see a "lie."
- **Feed the Loop:** Use destination failures to improve upstream logic and source contracts.

CHAPTER 19

Communicating with Code

In this chapter, we pivot from the "infrastructure" to the "alphabet." In a high-pressure data environment, code isn't just a set of instructions for a computer; it is a communication tool between human beings. We explore why "clever" code is the enemy of reliability, the power of standardized linting, and how consistent style acts as a psychological safety net during a crisis.

The Legend of the "Enigma Script"

I once inherited a data pipeline responsible for calculating the daily "Risk Score" for a fintech startup. The engineer who wrote it was a self-described "wizard." He prided himself on efficiency and "minimalism." The core of the pipeline was a single 400-line SQL query with 15 nested subqueries, 0 aliases, and variables named a, b, $c1$, and $temp$. There wasn't a single comment in the file. On his last day, the wizard told me, "It's optimized for the compiler; the engine handles it perfectly."

Three weeks later, the "Risk Score" for every user suddenly dropped to zero. I needed six hours staring at that script, trying to deconstruct the "wizardry." Because the code was unreadable, I couldn't tell if a logic error was a bug or a deliberate feature of the model. I ended up rewriting the entire thing from scratch just to understand it.

The wizard's code was "performant," but it was fundamentally **unreliable** because it was **unmaintainable**. In the RDPF, we believe that **if a human cannot easily read code, it cannot be trusted by the business.**

Readability as a Reliability Feature

In software engineering, there is a famous saying: *"Code is read ten times more often than it is written."* In a data platform, this ratio is even higher. During an incident, every second you spend trying to figure out what a variable means is a second the business is losing money. Standardized code style isn't about "looking pretty"; it's about **reducing cognitive load.** When every script in your platform follows the same structure, your brain stops "translating" the syntax and starts "understanding" the logic. Reliability is found in the **transparency** of your intent.

The Linter as the Law

We don't leave code style to "personal preference." Personal preference leads to "Style Wars" and inconsistent repositories. Instead, we use **Automated Linters and Formatters.**

For Python, we use Black (the uncompromising code formatter) and Flake8. For SQL, we use SQLFluff. These tools are integrated into the **CI/CD Pipeline**. If your code doesn't meet the styling standards, the pipeline rejects it before it even reaches the human review stage. This removes the "ego" from the process. It's not a senior engineer telling you your code is messy. It's a machine telling you it's inconsistent.

The Map of Meaning (Naming Conventions)

The most difficult part of data engineering is naming things. But in a reliable platform, we use a **Map of Meaning** to ensure names are descriptive and predictable.

Bad Name	Good Name	Why?
df1	raw_orders_df	**Context:** We know exactly what is inside.
tmp_tbl	stg_ecommerce_sales	**Origin:** We know where it came from and its layer (Staging).
calc_val	is_premium_customer	**Boolean:** Use "is_" or "has_" to signal a True/False flag.
1.15	VAT_RATE_GERMANY	**Constants:** No "Magic Numbers"; names should reveal intent.

By using clear names, you turn your code into **Self-Documenting Logic.** A new engineer should be able to read your script and understand exactly which data is moving through the pipes without needing a separate Word document.

Modularization vs. The "God Script"

A "God Script" is a single file that tries to do everything: ingestion, cleaning, transformation, and uploading. God Scripts are reliability nightmares. If one part breaks, the whole thing is a mystery.

In the RDPF, we follow the **Single Responsibility Principle**:

- One function = One task.
- One script = One logical step in the DAG.

By breaking your code into small, modular pieces, you make it **testable**. It is easy to write a unit test for a 10-line function that calculates tax; it is nearly impossible to test a 1,000-line script that does "everything."

The Narrative of the Code (Commenting)

If code is the "what" of your platform, comments are the **"why."** Computers don't read comments, but the engineer who has to fix your pipeline at 3:00 AM certainly does. In a reliable system, the "why" is often more important than the "how."

Commenting provides **Contextual Safety**. It ensures that specific business logic, "weird" edge cases, and the historical reasons for a certain transformation are preserved. It prevents a future engineer from "fixing" code that looks like a mistake but is actually a deliberate workaround for an upstream quirk. The most common mistake is writing comments that simply repeat the code.

Bad: df = df.filter(df.age > 18) # Filter users where age is greater than 18

Good: df = df.filter(df.age > 18) # Exclude minors to comply with GDPR restrictions

- **The Docstring:** Every modular function should have a standardized header (Docstring) explaining its purpose, inputs, outputs, and assumptions.
- **Standardized Tags:** Use TODO: for planned improvements, FIXME: for known issues needing a permanent fix, and HACK: for necessary but "dirty" solutions caused by external limitations.
- **SQL Inline Comments:** SQL can quickly become a "Wall of Text." Use inline comments to explain the logic of complex joins or filters step by step.

Code style is finalized in the **Peer Review**. This isn't just a "gatekeeper" moment; it's a knowledge-transfer session. A reliable peer review asks:

- "Could I maintain this if the author vanished tomorrow?"
- "Are the 'Why' comments present for any weird edge cases?"

Consistency across the team creates a **Collective Ownership** mindset, where everyone is responsible for the health of the codebase.

Key Takeaways

- **Prioritize Clarity over "Wizardry":** If code is hard to read, it is inherently hard to trust.
- **Automate Enforcement:** Let linters handle the "Style Wars" so the team can focus on logic.
- **Name with Intent:** Use descriptive names that reveal the "Map of Meaning" inside the data.
- **Avoid "God Scripts":** Modularize code into small, testable, single-purpose functions.
- **Comment the "Why":** Use comments to explain the business context and edge cases, not the syntax.
- **Keep Comments Fresh:** A stale comment is a lie; if the logic moves, the comment must follow.

CHAPTER 20

Documenting

In this last technical chapter, we address the most neglected pillar of reliability: **Documentation**. In most companies, documentation is a "Museum of Ancient History," enriched with a collection of dusty Wiki pages and PDFs that were accurate for exactly twenty minutes and have been lying to engineers ever since. We explore why "Static Documentation" is a liability, how to build "Living Documentation," and why the best manual is the one that is written into the code itself.

The "Bus Factor" Crisis

I once visited a logistics firm where the entire data platform was held together by a single engineer called Greg. He was a genius, but he was also an "Information Silo." He had no documentation because, in his words, "It's all in my head, and I'm faster without it."

By Tuesday, Greg didn't show up; he went on a family holiday and moved to an island with no cell service. A critical pipeline failed. The team spent three days trying to find where the credentials were stored, how the tables were joined, and who the business contact was for the source API. The "Bus Factor" (the number of people who need to get hit by a bus to kill the project) was exactly **one**. Because Greg hadn't documented his work, his "efficiency" cost the company hundreds of thousands of dollars in downtime. If knowledge exists only in a human brain, the platform is unreliable and becomes a hostage.

Documentation as Code

In the RDPF, **Reliability is the absence of secrets.** A reliable platform doesn't just have "one big document." It has three distinct tiers of information tailored to different audiences:

Tier	Target Audience	Purpose	Tooling
The Glossary	Business Stakeholders	Defining what metrics mean (e.g., "What is a 'Net Sale'?")	Data Catalog / Wiki
The Architecture	New Engineers	High-level "How it works" and infrastructure maps.	READMEs / Diagrams
The Metadata	Automated Systems	Schema details, lineage, and constraints.	dbt / Swagger / Catalogs

The reason documentation fails is that it lives in a different place than the code. An engineer changes the code in GitHub but forgets to update the page in Confluence.

We solve this by using **Documentation as Code**.

- **README.md:** Every repository must have a README.md file in the root folder. This file explains how to set up the environment, how to run tests, and what the code's purpose is.
- **Inline dbt Docs:** If you use a tool like dbt, your column descriptions live inside the .yml files right next to your SQL.

When documentation is part of the code, it undergoes the same **Peer Review** (Chapter 19) as the logic. If you change a column but don't update the description in the code, the reviewer rejects the Pull Request. This ensures the documentation evolves at the same speed as the platform.

The "Readme-First" Development

Before you write a single line of logic, you should write the **README**. This is a psychological trick that forces you to define the "Goal" and the "Interface" of your task before you get bogged down in the syntax.

A "Readme-First" approach ensures that you are building something that makes sense. If you can't explain what the script does in three sentences in a README, the logic is likely too complex and needs to be modularized (Chapter 19).

The Automated Lineage Map

As we discussed in Chapter 12 (Observability), manually drawing "Data Flow Diagrams" is a waste of time. They are out of date the moment you hit "Save."

Reliable documentation uses **Automated Lineage**. Tools like dbt or DataHub scan your code and database logs to generate a map for you. This is the "Truth" of the platform. It doesn't tell you what the engineer *thought* happened. It tells you what the system is *actually* doing.

The Discovery Layer

For your business stakeholders, the "Code" is a black box. They need a **Discovery Layer**. A Data Catalog acts as a "Search Engine" for your data.

- *"Where is the table for 'Customer Churn'?"*
- *"Who is the owner of the 'Sales' dataset?"*
- *"Is this table 'Production-Ready' or is it an 'Experimental' draft?"*

The discovery layer includes business value descriptions, requirements clarifications, a solution overview, pipeline architecture, and descriptions of data products. It should include links to related stories on task management systems and code repositories.

By providing this layer, you reduce the "interruptions" to the engineering team. Reliability is also about protecting the engineers' time so they can focus on hardening the platform rather than answering the same "Where is the data?" questions every day.

Key Takeaways

- **Secrets are Risks:** If only one person knows how it works, it is broken by design.
- **Keep it Near the Code:** Use README.md and inline comments so the documentation lives where the work happens.
- **Automate the Maps:** Never draw a manual data flow diagram if a tool can do it for you.
- **Document the "Why":** Focus on the business context that isn't obvious from looking at the code.
- **The "Readme-First" Rule:** Define the destination before you start the journey.
- **Empower the Stakeholders:** Use a Data Catalog to turn your platform from a "Black Box" into a searchable library.

CHAPTER 21

Promoting Reliability

In this chapter, we move beyond the code, the pipelines, and the automated tests. We have built a world-class engine, but an engine is only as good as the team that maintains it. Reliability is a **cultural choice,** not a technical specification. We will explore the "Blame Game" vs. "Blamelessness," the danger of the "Hero Culture," and how to build a psychological safety that allows your team to innovate without fear. This is the "Human Operating System" that keeps the platform running when the scripts reach their limit.

The Executive Who Wanted a "Head on a Plate"

I once worked for a retail company that suffered a massive data failure during its biggest sale of the year. A misconfigured cloud permission had locked the "Gold" tables, leaving the marketing team flying blind for four hours.

The following Monday, the VP of Engineering called a meeting. He didn't ask how to fix the permissions or how to automate the check. He looked around the room and asked, "*Whose fault was this? I want a name. I want accountability.*"

The room went silent. The engineer who had made the mistake shrank into their chair. From that day on, the culture changed. No one took risks. No one proposed new features. Everyone was so afraid of being "the one to blame" that the platform stopped evolving.

By demanding a "head on a plate," the VP had traded the long-term reliability of the system for a moment of short-term ego. In the RDPF, we believe that **every "human error" is actually a system failure.** If a single person can break the platform, the platform was already broken. It just happened to be the one to prove it.

The Blameless Post-Mortem

The cornerstone of a reliability culture is the **Blameless Post-Mortem**. When something goes wrong, the goal is to conduct a "Digital Autopsy" without looking for a villain.

The Rules of the Blameless Post-Mortem

1. **Assume Good Intent:** Everyone came to work to do a good job. No one *tried* to break the database.

2. **Focus on the "How," not the "Who":** Instead of "Dave pushed the code," we say "The CI/CD pipeline allowed a script with a null-pointer to reach production."

3. **Identify the System Gap:** Why was there no guardrail? Why didn't the alert fire sooner?

4. **Publish the Results:** Share the findings with the whole company. Transparency builds trust and prevents other teams from making the same mistake.

When you remove the fear of punishment, people become incredibly honest. And when people are honest, you find the root cause ten times faster.

Killing the "Hero Culture"

Many teams have a "Hero" who stays up all night, knows every secret of the code, and "saves the day" during every outage. While heroes are impressive, they are a **Reliability Risk.**

Why Hero Culture is Toxic:

- **Burnout:** Heroes eventually break.

- **Knowledge Silos:** Information stays in the Hero's head (the "Bus Factor" from Chapter 20).

- **Delayed Automation:** If a Hero can fix it manually in five minutes, the team never feels the "pain" required to automate the fix properly.

A reliable culture values **Sustainable Excellence** over individual heroics. We celebrate the person who writes the script that prevents the 2:00 AM wake-up call, not just the person who answers the phone. We move from "I fixed it" to "We hardened root cause solution."

The Andon Cord Mentality

Borrowed from the Toyota Production System, the **Andon Cord** is a physical cord that any worker on the assembly line can pull to stop the entire factory if they see a defect.

In a data platform, we need a **Cultural Andon Cord**. Any engineer, regardless of seniority, should have the authority to "Stop the Line" if they see a reliability risk.

- *"I'm not comfortable deploying this feature because the tests are flaky."*
- *"We need to stop new development for a week to fix the Documentation Debt."*

In a weak culture, this is seen as "slowing things down." In a reliability culture, this is seen as **saving the company from a future catastrophe.**

SLOs as a Shield, Not a Weapon

In Chapter 13, we discussed **Service Level Objectives (SLOs)**. In many companies, SLOs are used as a weapon to punish teams that miss their targets. In the RDPF, the SLO is a **Shield**.

If the team has a 99.9% SLO and they are currently at 99.95%, the "Shield" is up. They have an **Error Budget** to spend. They can take risks, try a new experimental engine, or ship a major architecture change.

If the SLO drops to 99.8%, the "Shield" is down. The budget is spent. The culture dictates that **all new feature work stops** until the reliability is restored. The SLO is the objective "third party" that decides the team's priorities, removing the emotion and the politics from the decision. **Reliability is a balance of power.** It is the agreement between the business (which wants features) and engineering (which wants stability) to respect the math of the Error Budget.

Psychological Safety and the "Stupid" Question

Data engineering is complex. No one knows everything. A reliable culture is one where asking a "stupid" question is encouraged.

- *"I don't understand how this join works."*
- *"Why are we using this specific API version?"*

When people feel safe to admit they don't know something, they catch errors before they are committed to code. When people pretend to understand to avoid looking "un-senior," errors flourish. Reliability is built on a foundation of **intellectual humility.**

Key Takeaways

- **Blame is a Distraction:** Focus on the system failure, not the human actor.
- **Retire the Heroes:** Automate knowledge and processes so the system doesn't rely on a single person's stamina.
- **Pull the Cord:** Empower everyone to prioritize quality over speed when the platform is at risk.
- **Spend Your Error Budget:** Use SLOs to decide when to innovate and when to stabilize.
- **Cultivate Humility:** Build a team where the "Stupid Question" is the most valuable tool in the room.
- **Reliability is a Practice:** It is not a destination; it is the daily commitment to the "Mirror of Truth."

CHAPTER 22

Continuing Great Work

We have spent twenty-one chapters dissecting the anatomy of a Reliable Data Platform. We've looked at the skeleton (Architecture), the nervous system (Alerting), the immune system (Auto-Testing), and even the soul (Culture). But a collection of organs isn't a person, and a list of features isn't a platform. In this final recap, we assemble the "Master Blueprint" of how these pieces interact to create a system that doesn't just survive but thrives under pressure.

You have reached the end of the manual, but the work of a data engineer is never truly "done." It is a continuous practice of stewardship. To wrap up the **Reliable Data Platform Framework (RDPF)**, we consolidate twenty-one chapters of technical rigor into five core values.

This Manifesto is your North Star. When the architecture gets messy, when the budget gets tight, or when the stakeholders are shouting for speed, return to these principles.

I. Truth Over Ease

We will never sacrifice the accuracy of the **Mirror of Truth** for the convenience of a quick fix. If the data is wrong, we hide it. If the logic is flawed, we fix it. We acknowledge that a "reliable" system that delivers the wrong answer is simply a high-speed machine for making bad decisions.

II. Systems Over Heroes

We reject the **Hero Culture**. We do not celebrate the midnight save; we celebrate the automated check that made the save unnecessary. We document our secrets, automate our recoveries, and ensure that the platform's survival never depends on the stamina of a single human being.

III. Clarity Over Cleverness

We write code for our colleagues and our future selves, not for our egos. We prioritize readability, modularity, and explicit commenting. We understand that "clever" code is a liability, while **clear code** is an asset that grows in value over time.

IV. Progress Over Perfection

We embrace the **Error Budget**. We do not aim for 100% uptime, because 100% is the enemy of innovation. We use our reliability as a foundation to take calculated risks, knowing that our guardrails, such as the airlocks, the circuit breakers, and the auto-tests, will catch us if we fall.

V. Empathy Over Blame

We treat every failure as a gift of information. We conduct **Blameless Post-mortems** because we value the health of our team as much as the health of our databases. We understand that psychological safety is the most critical component of a high-performance platform.

The End of the Journey

The journey comes to an end with the **Reliable Data Platform Framework**. We have moved from requirements understanding, environments, and source ingestion to destination checks, from code style to CI/CD, and from alert to smart recovery.

But as you close this book, remember that tools will change, but Idempotency, Observability, Blamelessness, and Business Alignment are eternal principles of reliability. A reliable platform is never "finished." It is a living, breathing entity that reflects the values of the people who build it.

The paradox of a truly reliable platform is what makes your job look easy. When everything works, stakeholders might wonder what you do all day. They don't see the thousands of "Silent Saves" performed by the circuit breakers that prevented meltdowns or the idempotent scripts that handled a midnight server crash without a single human waking up. Always remember, **your success is measured by the absence of drama**.

Index

accountability, 81, 132
accounting, 114
Actionable Alerting, 81
adapt, 96
Agile, 33, 110
Airlock Principle, 46
Alert Fatigue, 80, 81
algorithm, 113
Amazon Web Services (AWS), 105
analysis, 103
analyst, 14, 66
analytics, 63
Anonymization, 44
Application Programming Interface (API), 5, 25, 38, 47, 49, 54, 75, 79, 81, 84, 90, 105, 117, 126, 135
architectural decision, 13
artifact, 102, 106
atomic, 17, 24, 62, 74, 75, 76, 109
atomicity, 24, 27
audit, 5, 15, 32, 40, 69, 82, 85, 106, 116, 118
backup, 37, 90
benchmark, 36, 40
BigQuery, 67, 92
blueprint, 23, 27, 35, 137
Boolean, 121
Boring Technology, 29, 34, 36
bug, 32, 34, 37, 48, 82, 89, 92, 98, 106, 120
Bulletproof Design, 23, 26
business decision, 23, 117
Business Intelligence (BI), 69
business leader, 73
business stakeholder, 126, 128
business strategy, 13, 18, 21, 23, 39, 62, 64, 69, 70, 76, 84
business value, 128
Central Processing Unit (CPU), 53, 66, 78, 79
centralized, 32, 76
CEO, 3, 13, 56, 113, 117
Change Failure Rate (CFR), 108
Chief Executive Officer (CEO), 3, 13, 56, 113, 117
Chief Financial Officer (CFO), 22
Chief Technology Officer (CTO), 77
Clock Drift, 75
cloud, 22, 33, 37, 38, 39, 44, 49, 50, 51, 66, 73, 75, 92, 131
Cognitive Load, 109
competitive advantage, 37
compiler, 120
compliance, 23, 63
contextual, 123

Continuous Integration and Continuous Deployment (CI/CD), 45, 46, 52, 100, 102, 104, 105, 106, 111, 121, 133, 140
cost, 7, 8, 9, 11, 13, 35, 37, 40, 69, 70, 71, 76, 126
CREATE TABLE, 92
Critical Path, 62, 63, 64
culture, 4, 9, 131, 132, 133, 134, 135, 137, 138
Customer Relationship Management (CRM), 60
dashboard, 4, 11, 12, 21, 25, 43, 54, 57, 68, 77, 79, 81, 85, 86, 90, 107, 110, 117
data architect, 15
data catalog, 126, 128, 129
data consumer, 13, 14
data contract, 57, 58
data engineer, 1, 4, 7, 12, 21, 24, 33, 36, 38, 42, 44, 45, 47, 48, 54, 67, 72, 74, 80, 97, 101, 114, 121, 135, 137
data engineering, 4, 7, 12, 24, 36, 38, 42, 44, 45, 48, 54, 67, 72, 74, 80, 97, 101, 114, 121, 135
data flow, 60, 64, 108, 128, 129
Data Flow Diagram (DFD), 128, 129
data leader, 5
Data Masking, 44
data mesh, 32, 33
data model, 33
data modeling, 33
data pipeline, 1, 11, 13, 14, 50, 60, 68, 78, 106, 119
data platform, 7, 9, 59, 71, 75, 85, 109, 120, 125, 134
data product, 129
data project, 18
data quality, 6, 32, 56, 86, 97
data scientist, 14
data system, 1
data team, 13
data warehouse, 47
database, 14, 26, 31, 34, 36, 44, 48, 49, 51, 66, 78, 81, 84, 93, 96, 102, 105, 116, 128, 133, 139
database schema, 14
Databricks, 92
data-driven, 1, 2, 3, 4
dataset, 30, 51, 98, 128
Day Zero, 5
dbt, 33, 99, 126, 127, 128
debugging, 2, 7, 25, 51, 81
decimal, 17
Defensive Ingestion, 55
Defensive Programming, 26
definitions, 17, 18, 19
Deployment Frequency (DF), 108
developer, 44, 45, 50, 102, 103
DevOps, 30, 108
Directed Acyclic Graph (DAG), 59, 60, 61, 62, 64, 82, 122
ecosystem, 13, 38
email, 97, 111, 116

entity, 140
Excel, 16, 30
Extract-Load-Transform (ELT), 33
Extract-Transform-Load (ETL), 33, 35
Fan-In, 62, 64
Fan-Out, 62
Fivetran, 33
foreign key, 116
fraud detection, 69
Freshness Check, 55
Functional Programming (FP), 38
General Data Protection Regulation (GDPR), 123
graph database, 29
Green Dashboard, 77
High Throughput Strategy, 69
High-Water Mark (HWM), 26
Horizontal Scaling, 66
Human Resources (HR), 5
Idempotent, 91
immutable, 50
Infrastructure as Code (IaC), 44, 47, 49, 52
internet, 1
Java, 36
JavaScript Object Notation (JSON), 39
Kafka, 29
Key Performance Indicator (KPI), 17, 72
Kubernetes, 29, 50
Lead Time for Changes (LT), 108
legacy data, 36
lineage, 80, 81, 82, 126, 128
LinkedIn, 30
Low Latency Strategy, 69
Machine Learning (ML), 1, 13
materialized view, 69
medallion architecture, 25, 32
metadata, 57, 117, 126
metrics, 13, 16, 17, 18, 39, 40, 68, 70, 79, 82, 107, 108, 126
microservices, 90
Midnight Ghost, 71, 72
Minimum Viable Requirement, 16
Modular, 61
modularity, 138
Network Time Protocol (NTP), 76
node, 68, 70
orchestration, 6, 59, 60, 62
Partition Pruning, 67
password, 45, 103, 105, 106
Personally Identifiable Information (PII), 99
Playback Technique, 15
Point-in-Time Recovery, 92
Postgres, 37
Process Shadowing, 16
product, 32
programming, 36
Python, 37, 49, 121
Quarantine Pattern, 56
Quarantine Table, 56

Redis, 69
referential integrity, 118
Requirement Contract, 17, 19
Resilient Programming, 26
Resume-Driven Development (RDD), 30
scalable, 32
sentiment analysis, 13
Service Level Agreement (SLA), 70, 75, 76, 85
Service Level Indicator (SLI), 84
Service Level Objective (SLO), 84
Single Source of Truth, 49
Slack, 80, 81, 83, 85
Snowflake, 33, 67, 92
social media, 57
Software as a Service (SaaS), 33, 37
software engineering, 80, 120
Spark, 35, 49, 67
Spiderweb, 59, 61
StackOverflow, 36
State Management, 26
strategy, 13, 18, 23, 35, 40, 57, 63, 74, 75, 86, 104, 107
technical debt, 12, 14
Temporal Mismatch, 72
Test-Driven Development (TDD), 95
Testing Pyramid, 95, 96
token, 34, 36
Vertical Scaling, 66
Watermark, 74

www.ingramcontent.com/pod-product-compliance
Lightning Source LLC
LaVergne TN
LVHW022223200926
848481LV00006B/2093
9798898161231